DONA[

HE HAD
RARE LIGHTS:
A BIOGRAPHY OF
WILLIAM WALLACE LINCOLN

outskirts
press

Outskirts Press, Inc.
http://www.outskirtspress.com

ISBN: 978-1-9772-0706-7

Cover photograph of Willie Lincoln colorized by *Ashley,* courtesy of the author.

Back cover photo of the author courtesy of the author.

Some of the material in this work appeared previously in *Mystic Chords of Memory: The Lost Journal of William Wallace Lincoln,* © 2009, 2012 by Donald Motier.

For Dr. Wayne C. Temple
Leading living authority
on Abraham Lincoln and his family.

Books by Donald Motier:

FICTION

Just Friends: A Novella and Two Short Stories (1984)
Just Friends, A Love Story (2003)
Unfinished Business (2003)
Return To Sonville (2005)
The Book of Joel (2005)

FACTION/HISTORICAL FICTION

Mystic Chords of Memory: The Lost Journal of William Wallace Lincoln (2009)
Saving Lincoln: Mystic Chords of Memory Part 2 (2014)

POETRY

Faces of Being (1971)
On the Hound and Other Prose-Poems 1970-78 (1978)
Mnemonicons: Prose Poems 1979-1990 (1991)
Co-Incidings: Collected Poems 1965-1991 (2001)
New Poems 2000-2008 (2009)

ACKNOWLEDGEMENTS

First and foremost I want to thank my research assistant, Fred K. Owens, for his persistence in ferreting out details of the life of Willie Lincoln from obscure contemporary sources and the often times frustrating online, phone and mail searches he diligently pursued. Dr. Wayne C. Temple, retired Deputy Director of the Illinois State Archives has been a continued inspirational and enthusiastic supporter of my research and has been invaluable in correcting factual errors as has Dr. James Cornelius, Curator of the Abraham Lincoln Presidential Library. Dorothy Zakkowski of the Sag Harbor, NY Historical Society provided the obituaries, list of burials and photographs of the grave stones of Taft family members buried in Oakland Cemetery.

Staff of the following museums, libraries and institutions for their copies of Willie's letters, articles and photographs, etc.: Abraham Lincoln Presidential Library and Museum, Illinois State Archives, Lincoln Library (Springfield), Sangamon County Historical Society, Lincoln Home National Historic Site, National Park Service (Springfield), Lincoln College Library and Museum (Lincoln, IL), Lincoln Heritage Public Library (Dale, IN), Lincoln Museum (Ft. Wayne, IN closed, now in the collection of The Allen County Public Library (Ft. Wayne), Chicago History Museum, Chicago Public Library, University of Chicago Library, University of Illinois, Chicago Library, Rockford

Public Library (IL), Champaign Public Library (IL), Urbana Free Library (IL), White House Historical Association, Martin Luther King, Jr. Memorial Library (Washington D.C.), Library of Congress, National Archives, Abraham Lincoln Library & Museum (Harrogate, TN), National Park Service, (Washington D.C.), Office of the County Historian, Wayne County, (NY), Sag Harbor Public Library & Historical Society (NY), Harvard University Library, New York Public Library, New York State Library, Long Branch Free Public Library (NJ), Pasadena Public Library (CA), Niagara Falls Museum (ON), Friends of Hildene, Manchester, (VT), Lancaster County Historical Society (PA), Carlisle Barracks Military History Library (PA), University of Nebraska Press (Lincoln), Pennsylvania State Archives, State Library of Pennsylvania, Historical Society of Dauphin County (Harrisburg), Ancestry.com, Findagrave.com

Also, the following individuals: Drs. John & Elva Winter, the late David Herbert Donald, William B. Bushong, the late Mrs. Willoughby T. Davis (granddaughter of Willie Taft), Jerry A. McCoy, Dr. Bryon Andreasen, Janet Birckhead, John Sellers, William Jamieson, Phil Wagner, Jennifer Ericson, Alice David, Elizabeth Flygare, Erin Tikovitch, Ron J. Keller, Kathryn Blackwell, Michael Sherbom, Evan Lattimer, Hillary Crehan, Susan M. Haake, Gloria Swift, Michelle Duell, Richard L. Baker, Mark Greek, Jason Meyers, Norma Bean, Jean H. Lythgoe, Christine Colburn, Arthur B. House, Jr., Jane Milem, Elaine Maruhn, Donna Aschenbrenner.

TABLE OF CONTENTS

Introduction

I PREVIOUSLY PUBLISHED two works of historical fiction or "faction" ("type of literature in which real events are used as a basis for a fictional story," *Pocket Oxford American Dictionary, second edition,* 2008, p, 284): *Mystic Chords of Memory: The Lost Journal of William Wallace Lincoln* (2009, 2012) and *Saving Lincoln: Mystic Chords of Memory Part 2* (2014) that were meant to honor the life of Willie Lincoln and suggest what both he and his father may have accomplished had they lived.

While doing the research for the above two volumes, I tracked down everything that was ever written about Willie as well as everything he was alleged to have said, written and done in his short remarkable life.

The following biography includes only the factual accounts of Willie's life from primary and secondary contemporary sources that are listed in the bibliography in the back of the text.

I recently was able to prove that I am related to Mary Lincoln through my great-great-great grandfather Nicholas Boyd (1772 - December 20, 1840) who married Mary Porter (January 1, 1781 - March 8, 1839), a daughter of Mary Todd's great-grandfather Revolutionary War General Andrew Christy Porter (September 24, 1743 - November 16, 1813) who is buried in Harrisburg Cemetery and whose estate was near Nicholas Boyd's in southern Lancaster County. William Wallace Lincoln is my *3rd cousin 2x removed, a connection I'd always intuitively and emotionally felt but had not proven till now. The complete family tree is listed in the addenda as is proof that both Nicholas, Andrew and his brother William were slave owners in the late 1700s and early 1800s in Pennsylvania, knew each other and sold human beings and goods to each other even though slavery was technically abolished in Pennsylvania in *1780.

*Both the current Ancestry.com list Willie as my 3rd cousin 2x removed, and the 2008 CD version Lite Family Tree Maker by Ancestry.com.

*Actually known as the Gradual Emancipation Act of 1780, there were several steps over the following years before full emancipation in Pennsylvania. Evidently, my 4th, and 3rd great-grandfathers respectively, took advantage of the "gradual aspect"…a sad commentary on them.

PREFACE

"Willie has rare lights…rare lights!"

ABRAHAM LINCOLN SAID to his secretary John Hay November 4, 1861 after the publication of Willie's poem "Lines on the Death of Colonel Baker" in the Washington newspaper *National Republican*.

"The short life of William Lincoln has been given little attention in the biographies of his father, or in other writings on the Lincoln family. In 1850, in the Lincoln home in Springfield, Illinois, there came, just four days before Christmas [December 21, the winter solstice] a real live Christmas present, a baby boy. This child was named William Wallace, after his Uncle Dr. William Smith Wallace who married Mary Lincoln's sister Frances Todd. He was, of course, promptly called Willie."

> - From "Willie Lincoln as Boy of Letters"
> by Charlotte A. Dubois in a magazine
> titled *The Power of the Written Word,*
> *Illinois State Register* (Springfield)
> August 22, 1922.

Since that article was published in 1922 by Charlotte Dubois whose family were neighbors and friends of the Lincolns in Springfield,

Ruth Painter Randall and Julia (Taft) Bayne have published books that do shed some light on Willie's life but do not give Willie his due as a remarkably gifted boy, the favorite of his father and indeed most like him in temperament, intelligence, empathy and wit.

Willie's life may seem too short to many, but those whose lives were touched by his understood that the quality of a life far exceeds the quantity of time in which one lives it.

Springfield

December 21, 1850 - February 11, 1861

WILLIAM WALLACE LINCOLN was born on the winter solstice December 21, 1850 in the Lincoln home at 8ᵗʰ & Jackson Streets in Springfield, Illinois. Willie, as he was called all his short life, was named for his uncle Dr. William Smith Wallace (July 10, 1802 - May 23, 1867) who was born in Lancaster, Pennsylvania. He graduated from Jefferson Medical College in Philadelphia and practiced medicine in Lancaster till 1836 when he moved to Springfield and met Mary (Todd) Lincoln's sister Frances Todd (March 7, 1817 - August 14, 1899) whom he married on May 21, 1839. He became the Lincoln family doctor and took care of Willie and his brothers when they were sick, or his partner Dr Preston Heath Bailhache (February 21, 1835 - October 8, 1919) did when Dr. Wallace was away from Springfield.

Mary Lincoln reported that her son was a good baby but sick a lot with colic and held his breath till he turned blue ostensibly to get his mother's attention. When Willie was three and his mother was getting ready to give him a bath and left the room for a minute, Willie saw his chance and ran bare-naked out the door and down the street. Mary yelled for Abe who chased him down and finally caught him behind a fence in a green field. Abe picked him up and carried his son home on his shoulders both of them laughing,

In 1855 when Willie was four and brother Thomas "Tad" Lincoln (April 4, 1853 - July 15, 1871) was two, the boys would watch for Abe when he came home from work at his law office and run to meet him, swinging on his coattails as he approached the house. After supper the boys would climb all over him as he sat telling them wonderful stories about fighting Indians during the Black Hawk War of 1832. Abe joined the Illinois Militia as a volunteer April 21, 1832, never saw combat but served till July 10, 1832 [was elected captain his first month; then a private], trips down the Mississippi on flatboats to New Orleans and growing up in Kentucky in the woods. Sometimes he would have a game of blind man's bluff, played marbles with them and Abe was an excellent top spinner.

On Sunday morning Abe would put Willie and Tad in their little wagon and pull them down to his office. The boys were quite wild and undisciplined at the office, scattering books and papers, smashing pens, spilling ink and dipping their fingers in it to draw pictures on the desks and walls and made a mountain of books, inkstands, pens and ashes from the stove in a pile on the floor and danced on top of it. Then, pretending the pile was a fire, urinating on it. Abe never paid any attention to their mischief. However, Lincoln's law partner would scowl at the boys calling them "hellcats." Lincoln, whose father probably physically abused him and worked him like a slave, believed the boys should be loved and allowed to express themselves as they saw fit as long as no one was hurt.

Another time Abe was pulling Willie and Tad in their wagon and reading a book at the same time and Tad fell out crying and screaming but Lincoln never noticed. When Lincoln was concentrating on something, you could fire-off the loudest firecracker and he wouldn't have noticed. Willie's yelling and Tad's crying soon brought Mary Lincoln out of the house to see what the commotion was and she scolded Abe who was very apologetic, dusting off Tad who was none the worse for wear.

On Saturday mornings in the winter Lincoln would take the boys along to the market. Willie and Tad would run after him but it was hard for them to keep up with Abe as he took such long strides. This was about 1854-1855 and the boys were only four and two, Willie not turning five till December 21, 1855. Willie would ply his father with a thousand questions, the "whys" that kids of that age have out of infinite curiosity about the world. As Willie and Tad got older, Abe would take them for walks in the country around Springfield explaining such things as which animal made this or that track, identifying different bird's nests they saw along the way, lizards, insects, plants and other things the boys noticed and asked Abe about. The boys had lots of friends in the neighborhood; children of the Sprigg, Diller, Melvin, Wheelock and Remann families. Henry Christian Remann, Jr. (April 6, 1850 - January 6, 1915) lived down the street at 802 S. 8th Street. He was Willie's age and was in the same class with Willie at Miss Corcoran's (Mary Ann Corcoran (? - August 18, 1876) School at 7th and Edwards Streets. Willie's other best friend was Edward "Eddie" Rathbun, Jr. (1848 - 1862) even though he only lived in Springfield from 1856-1859. Eddie was living directly across 8th street from the Lincolns.

Willie and Tad loved to do pranks and one summer night after dark, Willie, Tad, Joe & Lincoln "Link" Dubois (1845 - March 3, 1926) hid behind Joseph "Joe" Kent's (May 1, 1847 - July 27, 1921) fence that bordered 8th Street and the sidewalk and with a long stick knocked off the hats of passers-by. Then they would quietly wait for another victim to pass by. Believing all danger of being caught had passed, they would creep forward again. One of the victims on that occasion proved to be Lincoln, but the boys didn't know who it was right away. They thought the victim had passed and were whispering trying to guess who it was and wondering if it was Lincoln when they suddenly heard, "Yes, boys it was Lincoln." Abe seemed to enjoy the prank but gently told them that the next man might not be so easy with them.

Sometimes Lincoln would collect all the kids in the neighborhood, put them in his big carriage and go out to the Sangamon River for picnics, fishing and swimming. Years later

in 1861 Willie would miss those great times at home in Springfield as there was no fishing or swimming in the dirty, polluted Potomac River and he and Tad weren't allowed near it.

When the circus came to Springfield every April, Lincoln would take the boys to see it. Abe seemed to enjoy it almost as much as the kids did, especially the clowns. How he would laugh. Sometimes Willie would forget he was his father and thought of him as just a "big kid."

After Abe had taken Willie and Tad to the circus, the boys decided to have their own circus parade with their friends, their friends' animals or their own and let them act. The boys wanted Mary Lincoln's sewing group who were meeting at the Lincoln home, to see the animals act. Each one of the boys held an animal. Willie let down his pet white rat on the floor first. The women began to hitch up their skirts and put up their feet and scream. Some even stood on their chairs. Then a boy let his turtle go. Some kittens came next. Next, a whole slew of chickens, one from each boy. A hop toad. A big bull frog croaking to go back to water. An old hen and Jim Crow [pet crow of Willie and Tad's] that repeated over and over, "Get out, ya bums!" At last some boy let down Willie and Tad's big black Tom cat. The women's screams scared Tom and he raced around the house and the other animals scattered. The women ran for the door, grabbed their sons and left. Tad and Aunt Emilie (Todd) Helm (November 11, 1836 - February 20, 1930) [coincidentally, she died at age 93 on the 68th anniversary of Willie's death] Mary Lincoln's half-sister laughed and laughed. Mary Lincoln grabbed Willie and screamed, "Why did you do such a thing to me?" Willie explained about their planned circus parade and how the animals were supposed to act and wanting the boys' mothers to see the show. Each animal was to have an act but they acted *better* than they taught them.

Mary Lincoln didn't answer.

So Willie said, "Well, father will laugh. He don't like a gang of women here all the time anyway."

That made Mary really mad and she yelled, "William Wallace! [she always called him that when mad at him] Did your father say that?"

Willie grinned and said, "No, mother. But I can tell when father doesn't like a thing. He's sad and quiet. But I'll bet he'll like our circus."

Sure enough when Lincoln came home and Mary told him about it, he yelled, "Good!" and laughed loud and long.

One day Ardelia Wheelock (Adelia [Wheelock] Sayres March 31, 1840 - 1923) [called Delie by Willie and Tad] who was the daughter of the Wheelocks who lived across the street from the Lincolns, had a taffy pull. Willie and Tad managed to get molasses all over themselves. Mary Lincoln was not happy as she as Abe were supposed to go to a reception at the Jesse Dubois home down the street that evening. Willie and Tad cried that they wanted to go too. Mary said no but Abe said OK if the boys stayed in the kitchen. The boys' older brother Bob (Robert Todd Lincoln August 1, 1843 - July 26, 1926) and Delie cleaned the boys up but got Tad's pants on backward and he yelled that he couldn't walk right and although he was supposed to stay in the kitchen during the reception, Tad snuck out but paid no attention to people's stares about his pants and generally made a nuisance of himself running around. Willie didn't mind staying in the kitchen as he got extra cake and fruit.

Mary Lincoln had a vegetable garden and Willie would help his mother pick tomatoes, squash and other vegetables and carry them into the kitchen where Mary and the neighbor ladies who helped her would pickle and preserve them. Willie and Tad were supposed to help tend the horses and clean the barn but Tad managed to disappear most of the time. Willie milked the Lincolns' cow Bossy while Bob would groom Abe's horses Old Buck or Old Bob if Lincoln was home.

In January of one year, 1855 or maybe 1856, there was a blizzard raging outside when Lincoln came home with something bulging in the front of his coat. A little whimper was heard and a small yellow head peeked out. It was a puppy and the boys named him Fido. It took a while but the Lincolns' four curious and jealous cats accepted this creature.

Mary Lincoln didn't like summer storms and the thunder and lightning frightened her and gave her headaches. Willie would make her special tea and hold her hand while she took her cordial [paregoric, a mixture of opium and alcohol] to soothe the pain. Lincoln was away on the circuit a lot during those times and Mary would sometimes ask an older neighbor boy, Joe Kent (Joseph Pillow Kent May 1, 1847 - July 27, 1921), who lived on the east side of Eighth Street to stay at the house.

When Lincoln was home and he didn't seem to notice the boys, Willie and Tad would stick him with Mary's hat pin, trip him when he was walking past or paste him with mud balls or other things to get his attention. Then he would *wake up*, take them for a walk, play piggyback or somersault

Lincoln had an addition put on the house in 1855-57 so that more people would fit in for the receptions, dinners, prominent guests and political talks.

In July of 1857 when Willie was six, Abe was home and the family took a long trip all the way to Niagara Falls, New York. They stayed at the Cataract House [July 24th]. It was very exciting for the boys to see all the water rushing over the falls and the people from all over the world who came to enjoy it. Willie, Tad and Bob particularly liked the museum on the Canadian side [July 25th] that had an Egyptian mummy and all manner of interesting oddities of nature. [Abe signed the guest book at the Niagara Falls Museum *A. Lincoln and Family* and it is in the possession of the current owner. On the same page is the signature of *P. T. Barnum*].

In the summer of 1857 Mary had a big party at the house and Willie and Tad noticed the men smoking and chewing tobacco. Early the next morning still in their nightshirts they snuck down to the kitchen and put licorice, paper and dried corn silk in their toy soap bubble pipes, lit them on the stove and pretended they were big men smoking tobacco and spitting black juice in the fire. However, "Aunt" Mariah (Bartlett) Vance (1819 - December 23, 1904), the Lincoln's Black housekeeper from 1850-1860 who had come in the kitchen to heat water to do wash in the shed, caught them. She yelled they'd burn down the house and that woke Mary who came running. Mary said that although the boys were only playing, they shouldn't model themselves after men who had bad habits pointing out that their father didn't smoke and didn't they want to please him. Of course they did and cleaned out their pipes and went back to making soap bubbles.

Later the boys went out to the back yard and climbed the wood-pile. Tad got a big splinter in his foot. Abe pulled out the splinter, washed his foot, put on some turpentine and wrapped it in a clean rag.

One weekend in September 1858 [September 25-28] when Lincoln was home from the campaign trail and speech making, he was upstairs soaking his tired, aching feet in a foot tub and Willie and Tad were playing around him. There was a knock on the door downstairs and Mary was busy in the kitchen preparing food for the visiting big-wigs, so Abe pulled his feet out of the tub, dried them, put on his slippers and went to answer it. Aunt Mariah came in the room and said the tub was in her way from cleaning. She left the room for a minute so the boys pulled the tub to the top of the stairs and pushed it over. When their mother and father came in the room to see what the noise was, the boys explained that besides helping Aunt Mariah by getting the tub out of her way, they thought about the trip to Niagara Falls last year and the *cat-racks* [cataracts] they saw made them want to make the *cat-racks*. The tub was just the boat bouncing on the rocks going over the falls. The boys had gone a little too far that day and Lincoln took them out to the shed in the back yard and locked them in with Jim Crow and the other pets till the company left.

In a little while Abe came out to the shed and let the boys out. Jim Crow screamed, "Come back! Come back!" He missed the boys when they were out of sight. Willie and Tad played palm ball [hand ball] and then went into the barn to play with their wooden wagon until dinner.

The whole Lincoln family loved cats. They had all kinds and colors. After Lincoln left for the office, Willie and Tad decided to take a mother cat and her kitten for a trip to see Bob who they thought was in school. They hitched two tom cats to their wagon and put mother and kitten in. Big mistake. The two toms took to fighting and the boys got scratched up pretty bad trying to separate them. They had blood all over their faces, arms and clothes torn. Aunt Mariah cleaned them up before Mary Lincoln saw them or she would have fainted.

When the boys had a cold Mary gave them vinegar tea made with sugar, red pepper, ginger and hot water.

Another time when Mary had a party for some women who like Mary were interested in spiritualism, the boys snuck downstairs in their red flannel nightshirts, went outside and played tick-tack on the window. Some of the ladies thought it was spooks. The boys also punched up through the bottom of chairs with darning needles so when they pulled the string the needle would pop up through the seat and stick anyone who sat down.

Willie first became interested in politics because he asked his father why he had to be away from home so much. Willie knew he was away a lot before because he was a lawyer and had to defend innocent people in courts around the state but now he said he was running for office. That was fine but Willie and the rest of the family missed him so much and Mary would get really upset when he was away too long. Lincoln explained that he had been nominated for Congress as a senator by the Republican Party that replaced the old Whig Party. Abe was nominated June 16, 1858 and had to leave home soon to travel around and make speeches and campaign. Abe made his famous "A House Divided Against Itself Cannot Stand" speech out loud to Willie and the family and Willie thought it was great although he didn't undersatnd all the words. Willie was only seven that summer, not turning eight till December 21. Willie accepted the fact that his father had to be away for the good of the country. From August through October of 1858 Abe traveled all over Illinois debating Stephen Arnold Douglas (April 23, 1813 - June 3, 1861); seven times in fact. Mary said she knew Douglas from the old days and that he was a good speaker but Abe was better. [What she didn't tell the boys was that she had been courted by Douglas at one time but chose Abe in the end]. Willie and the family anxiously awaited the election returns in November and although Lincoln lost, he had given the best speeches and was not discouraged.

Mary Lincoln was having another big party [she was always having them] and Willie, Tad and the other boys there decided to do a trick Abe played on Mary. The boys snuck around the backs of chairs and tied all the ribbons and sashes the ladies had strung from their hats and dresses to the backs of the chairs. They left the streamers loose but tied the knots tight. When the ladies moved or turned their heads too far, off popped their hats to one side or the other. Sometimes their bonnets fell to the floor. The streamers from their necks would choke them. Some of their sashes were pulled completely off when they got up from their chairs.

When Lincoln got home and was told about it he laughed and laughed and hugged Willie and Tad.

Once in the summer of 1859 Willie had been over at his friend Henry's [Remann] house playing and as it was very hot that day so they went back to Willie's house to get some of Mary Lincoln's lemonade. When they came in the door they found Mary shouting and Tad crying. That wasn't necessarily unusual as he often cried when he didn't get his way but this time his wails were different and louder. Lincoln happened to come in the door behind Willie and Henry and he too wondered what all the commotion was about saying, "What in tarnation has that boy done now?" When Abe, Willie and Henry got to the kitchen they saw Mary beating Tad's legs with a switch. Mary rarely beat Tad and never Willie. So Willie knew Tad had to have done something serious. It turned out Tad had lied about keeping a dime from the change Mary had sent him to the store with. Abe made Tad turn his pockets inside out and out fell the dime. Even though lying was something neither Abe or Mary tolerated, ever, Willie knew that his father did not approve of his mother beating Tad and red in face he leaned over Mary and looking in her eyes, said in a voice tender and gentle with understanding, "Mary! Mary!" As far as it is kown, Tad was never beaten again. Mary knew though Lincoln's words were gentle his red face meant he was angry and he rarely ever was but when he was you got out of his way. Lincoln had no tolerance for corporal punishment as he likely suffered from it from his own father.

As was mentioned previously, neighbor boy Joe Kent would ofter stay with the Lincoln family when Abe was away. Mary asked Mrs. Kent to let Joe help Willie and Tad [if he could be found] care for their carriage horse Old Buck and their cow Bossy since he was older and Bob was away at Phillips Exeter Academy. Old Bob [his real name was Robin but he was called Old Bob] was Abe's favorite horse and his riding horse. Also during that summer when Lincoln was home Link Dubois or one of the older neighborhood boys would persuade Joe Kent to ask Abe for the loan of Old Buck so the boys could then hitch him to Mr. Alsop's (Thomas Alsop December 28, 1815 - 1891) flour delivery wagon that would take them to Spring Creek to go swimming. The reason that they had to borrow Mr. Alsop's carriage was because Lincoln would not lend Joe his carriage telling him, "No, Joseph, There are two things I will not lend: my wife and my carriage."

Willie went to school at Miss Mary Ann Corcoran's School on the northeast corner of 7th and Edwards Street where Bob had attended. Willie went there for the first three grades before Lincoln was elected president [November 6, 1860] and the family moved to Washington. Willie loved school, especially reading, ciphering, history and geography. Miss Corocoran never had to use the "slipper" [instrument for paddling miscreants] on Willie. Another teacher of Willie's was Hester (Watson) Billson (July 21, 1826 - March 26, 1862), who taught piano and melodian [melodeon, a small reed organ popular in the 19th century] from 1854-57 on Market St. between 8th & 9th about a block from the Lincoln home. A widow, Mrs. Billson married Charles Reeves in 1857 and moved to Cleveland. We know Willie knew how to play the piano for on March 10, 1861 Willie was scolded by Cousin Lizzie (Elizabeth T. [Grimsley] Jacoby May 10, 1838 - October 2, 1878) for playing *aires* [popular tunes of the day] on the Sabbath in the Executive Mansion. At home Mary Lincoln taught the boys to memorize fairy tales such as "The Three Bears," little verses, the poems of Robert Burns and they read the novels of Sir Walter Scott. Willie's favorite was *Rob Roy* that he and Bob read several times. Tad didn't really learn much as he couldn't sit still and had a speech impediment [possibly a cleft palate] and was too young at that time anyway. Mary also taught the boys various children's dances and made them dance and recite poems to visitors to the boys' embarrasment.

Willie was interested in the same things Abe was. They both loved the railroad and Lincoln had been the solicitor for the Illinois Central Railraod that ran up to Chicago where it connected with railroads across the country. Since the railroad was constructed Lincoln could get home faster and not have to rely on horseback. Abe had bought Willie a new toy train for his birthday and he and Tad had a great time playing with it. Willie had fun making timetables and conducting his own imaginary trains from Springfield to Chicago to New York. In June of 1859 Lincoln had to try a case in Chicago and took Willie along. Willie was very excited and couldn't wait to go. It was his greatest adventure since the trip to Niagara Falls in July of 1857. The train whizzed along at the amazing speed of 30 miles per hour. The engine tooted and the smoke trailed by as Willie looked out at the green fields rushing by. They stayed at a big hotel called the Tremont House on Lake Street and they could see Lake Michigan from out the window. To Willie's eight-year-old eyes Chicago was a very beautiful town and so BIG. Willie met his father's adversary Stephen Douglas who was also staying at the Tremont. Douglas was very short. Willie wrote his best friend Henry Remann back in Springfield telling him about the Tremont and what he and his father did. Willie modeled his letter after the fairy tale that he and Henry had both loved when they were small, "The Three Bears." When Willie got home he asked Henry if he recognized it and Henry said he had and thought it was a nice idea.

The Lincoln family went to Sunday services at the First Presbyterian

Church in Springfield where they had rented their own family pew. Similarly, my great-great grandfather, Robert Powers, (1783 - March 25, 1850) who emigrated from Northern Ireland, rented family pew #121 at the First Presbyterian Church of Lancaster, Pennsylvania for $3 for 9 months in 1815. Lincoln started taking the family to church after the death of Edward "Eddy" Baker Lincoln (March 10, 1846 - February 1, 1850) of tuberculosis. Sometimes, after Sunday School or on days they didn't go to church, Willie would write little sermons and give them to his "congregation" that consisted of Mary, Tad, Julia Sprigg, Fido and the cats.

Fido, who grew into a mid-sized yellow dog, followed Lincoln and the boys everywhere; Abe, when he went to the market or when they all went to Diller's Drugstore. Mr. Diller's (Roland Weaver Diller October 5, 1822 - August 18, 1905) son Isaac (July 14, 1854 - September 28, 1943) was a year younger than Tad and one of the Lincoln boys best friends. Diller's is where the Lincolns would get their household supplies such as castor oil, coffee, sugar, soap, cologne, medicine, hair balsam, calomel, restorative, deadshot for killing bedbugs, and candy vanilla. On hot summer days Abe, Willie and Tad would go to Diller's and sit at the fountain and sip glasses of cool, fruit-flavored soda water which was new that year (1859). Fido also liked to follow Abe to the barbershop of Billy the Barber Florville (William Florville September 12, 1807 - April 13, 1868) and wait outside and greet other dogs as they passed by.

Willie spent a lot of time with his best friends Henry Remann and Eddie Rathbun. Henry liked school and liked to read as much as Willie did. [Henry would found the first public library in Springfield]. Henry had a little sister Josie (Josephine [Remann] Edwards April 28, 1842 - October 4, 1918) whom Lincoln adored probably because he never had any daughters. Lincoln loved all children and they loved him too. He put up rope-swings for them, let them sit on his tall shoulders [especially little Josie] so they could see when the circus parade came to Springfield every April, played marbles, told stories about bear hunts and the Indian [Black Hawk] War where he saw people scalped, and buried a family of scalping victims, and about the Mississippi River pirates he fought when they tried to steal his flatboat. He licked them good, too.

As mentioned, Henry Remann liked to read as much as Willie and Bob Lincoln, who had a lot of books, had promised to lend one to Henry telling him to come to the Lincolns' on a certain day. Unfortunately, Bob forgot and Willie and the boys had all gone swimming in Spring Creek. When they got back home, Abe told Willie that Henry had come over and asked about the book Bob was to lend him. Of course Henry was disappointed that Bob wasn't home so Abe took him into Bob's room [Willie and Tad shared a bedroom but Bob had his own since he was older] and gave him *Don Quixote* by Cervantes saying, "Every boy who desires a book should have one."

Another time that summer that Willie would never forget was when he took four cigars from one of the boxes of cigars that people were always giving his father. Tad, Fred Dubois (Fred Thomas Dubois May 29, 1851 - February 14, 1930) and Jesse Dubois (Dr. Jesse Kilgore Dubois November 1848 - October 30, 1908) were right behind Willie as he crept quietly out of the house to the backyard and barn. Willie showed the boys the cigars and matches but they all agreed it was too risky to smoke them there so they went up the alley to the barn of Mrs. Niles (Adelia D. [Salisbury] Niles March 9, 1830 - October 11, 1899) one of their neighbors and friends where they proceeded to light the cigars and have a good smoke, their first offense. A sicker lot of boys there never was and Willie was to blame. Their wails of woe brought out Mrs. Niles and she took the boys into her house, fixed them up as best she could in the way of allaying their sufferings and called for their respective mothers. When Mary Lincoln and Mrs. Dubois (Adelia [Morris] Dubois October 17, 1820 - October 18, 1886) saw the boys' agony, they were not even punished but received instead much undeserved sympathy. Willie never smoked again.

Lincoln was persuaded to run for the nomination for president by the Republican Party and was away for parts of August to mid-December 1859 making speeches in Iowa, Kansas, Wisconsin, Indiana and Ohio. Willie really missed him but understood how important the speeches were to get the nomination. Abe came home around the 15th of December and December 20th, the day before Willie's 9th birthday, Lincoln's campaign autobiography was sent to Jesse Weldon Fell (November 10, 1808 - February 25, 1887), who got it published. It told how Abe was born in a log cabin in Kentucky and about his early life there working hard for his father, his move to New Salem, Illinois, marrying Mary Todd on November 4, 1842 and move to Springfield.

Willie wanted a party for his 9th birthday so Mary sent out invitations to a whole lot of boys and girls. The invitation read, "Willie Lincoln will be pleased to see you Wednesday afternoon at 3 o'clock." Fifty or sixty boys and girls came and Mary had everything planned from the games played to the aires [songs] sung and refreshments served. The weather being cold a fire was burning in the front parlor stove. Several of the boys laid on the floor near the stove. As an amusement, they took straws from a nearby broom and touched the straws to the sides of the red-hot stove. The intense heat disintegrated the straws without producing a flame giving the illusion that they were passing through the metal wall of the stove. While it was not a scheduled party activity the boys enjoyed it. When the party was over Mary gave each of the guests a small favor to take home. Mary stood at the front door and bade farewell to each boy and girl with a handshake. Willie was very happy that his party was a great success and that so many boys and girls came. Not surprising though as Willie himself was very popular with his peers, and his father was loved by all of Springfield.

In January 1860 a very exciting, colorfully dressed young man named Elmer Ephraim Ellsworth (April 11, 1837 - May 24, 1861) and his boys did an exhibition drill in Springfield. He had visited the Lincolns a week or so earlier and they were all quite taken with him.

In February 1860 both Willie and Tad got sick with very bad colds. They got sick the Saturday night after Lincoln left on his speech-making tour up in New England. Both boys missed him very much when he was away, and Mary did too. Mary worried something bad would happen but Willie tried to tell her it will be alright and not to be afraid. Philip Dinkel (1845? - September 20, 1930) who was 15, came to stay with Mary and the boys while Abe was away to help with the animals. On February 27, Lincoln made his famous Cooper Union Speech that all the people loved and helped him get the nomination.

Abe would often take Willie and Tad along when he went to see Mr. Baker (Edward Lewis Baker June 3, 1829 - July 8, 1897) who was editor of the *Illinois State Journal* whose office was at 116 North 6th Street. Sometimes other men would come in and after they were done talking politics they would go out to the vacant lot immediately south of the office between Mr. Carmody's (John Carmody 1818 - April 1, 1903) liquor store and a clothing store. It was shut off from view of the street by a tight board fence. At the south end of a the block was the solid brick wall of a three story building. The men would play fives [early name for hand ball, also called palm ball for obvious reasons] hitting the ball with their hands against the wall. A chalk line had been drawn across the wall. Each side consisted of two players. The ball was made of rubber covered with twine and over that was leather sewed on tightly and as smoothly as possible. After the men were done playing, Willie, Henry, the Dubois boys and others would get up their own game. Tad tried to play but couldn't hit it right and got mad.

Springfield had a volunteer fire company and Willie and the boys got up their own company, but to run with a mere clothesline attached to mere air or at best a pumpless sulky borrowed from unguarded premises was not satisfying. It was a momentous discovery that at Withey's (George D. Withey May 21, 1827 - September 17, 1899) Carriage "repository" there was a force-pump on four wheels for garden service. It had only an ordinary pump handle. For a certain considerable sum Mr. Withey would substitute for this handle two brakes long enough for the hands of a dozen boys. He allowed the boys to test its pumping qualities and it was agreed it should be named

"The Deluge." It was decided to ask a quarter each from such house-holders that were deemed approachable to fund their service. Johnny Kaine (John Kane [not Kaine] (184? - February 12, 1864), one of the older boys among Willie's firemen, decided to approach Lincoln for a donation. When Colonel Ellsworth's Zouaves came to town [August 13] the boys lost interest in The Deluge and instantly became soldiers. Drums and wooden guns took the place of the red shirts and fire-fighting. John Kane, who was quite the talented drummer, became the drummer for the Zouaves. He later enlisted in the 72nd Illinois Infantry and died a private. He is buried in the Camp Butler National Cemetery in Springfield.

Lincoln became more famous after the Cooper Union Speech and gained the nomination for president May 18, 1860. Willie became more interested in politics then. Willie wrote his own little speeches and gave them to whomever would listen. Usually, it was Tad, Henry, Fido, Isaac Diller, other neighborhood boys and Delie. It was very exciting for Willie and Tad as the crowds cheered for their father. At noon on the day of the nomination there was a 100 gun salute and that night torch-light parades, bonfires and many vistitors came to the Lincoln home. Willie and Tad were standing on the front steps in their best pantaloons they wore for the occasion when a man who said he was Mr. Evarts (William Maxwell Evarts February 6, 1818 - February 21, 1901) of New York asked Willie, "Are you Mr. Lincoln's son?" "Yes, Sir!" Willie answered proudly. "Then let's shake hands," Evarts replied. Willie shook hands with the gentleman full of pride at being his father's son.

After all the crowd left, Willie and Tad tried to keep the dying embers of a bonfire in the street in front of their house going. Tad yelled, "I've got a good one [stick] Willie!" After Tad handed it to him Willie realized it was a picket from a neighbor's dooryard fence.

Willie made signs that had the slogan "Vote For Old Abe" and stood on the terrace urging passersby. Willie organized parades by neighborhood boys that ended up calling for a speech by Willie. Willie gladly obliged. Willie tried to be like his father, imitating his manner and gestures, carrying his head slightly tilted to the left and telling stories of Abe's that he remembered.

The excitement of that time was saddened by the death of Willie's ten-year-old cousin Clark Moulton Smith, Jr. (March 10, 1850 - June 12, 1860) of typhoid fever. He was the son of Mary's sister Ann (Ann Maria [Todd] Smith 1820 - March 21, 1891) and Clark Moulton Smith, Sr. (May 10, 1820 - July 28, 1885). Willie felt really sad for Clark's parents and would miss his cousin very much. The Lincoln family went to Clark's funeral the next day at the Smith home at 113 South 5th Street. Clark was very pale but looked just like he was sleeping. For a week or so afterwards Willie had nightmares about looking in the coffin and seeing himself there instead, much like the dream his father would have five years later. Willie would wake up with a start, heart pounding and drenched in sweat.

Then, about two weeks later Willie himself got sick. Dr Wallace said it was scarlet fever. Willie was scared he would die like Clark and was very sick for a month and couldn't get out of bed to see the crackers [firecrackers] being fired off on the 4th of July. [Having scarlet fever for longer than two weeks can, like rheumatic fever, damage the heart valves, and this could have contributed to Willie's inability to fight off the typhoid and small pox attack he suffered in February 1862]. Lincoln had been campaigning in Chicago and when he came back he showed Willie an article that had appeared on June 29th in the *Chicago Press & Tribune* that said Willie was ill and at the point of death. They not only had that wrong but said Willie was six and Lincoln's youngest child, confusing him with Tad. Abe told Willie that newspaper accounts are notoriously inaccurate. Willie didn't really feel well enough to go outside and play till July 17th. Finally, with half of his summer gone, Willie was able to go barefoot and run, play, swim and fish with the boys. What a relief it was for Willie to get out of that stuffy room.

After being sick for a month and not having any sweets, Willie woke up the next morning [July 18th] craving some candy. Mary said

Abe was at the State House so Willie ran over there and found his father talking to a man from Wisconsin named Mr. Bliss (John Spoor Bliss January 3, 1832 - May 9, 1891). Willie said, "Father, I want twenty-five cents." Abe asked Willie what he wanted it for and he replied, "I want to buy candy with it." Abe said, "I shall not give you twenty-five cents but five cents." Lincoln put the five cents on the desk. Willie was angry that his father only wanted to give him five cents and not taking it stormed out. As Abe surely knew, it did not take long for Willie to figure out the five cents was better than nothing, so Willie returned to the State House about ten minutes later and took the five cents telling his father thank you and smiling. Willie later felt bad because he hadn't even said please when he first asked his father and was a bit greedy [probably from being sick so long and thinking he deserved the money].

Near the end of July one of Bob's friends from Phillips Exeter Academy [the prep school Bob was forced to attend to gain enough credits to get into Harvard] came to Springfield to visit the Lincolns. This was most likely George Carlisle Latham (March 12, 1838 - April 13, 1911) who is listed in the student roster for Exeter for 1859-60 along with Bob.

Later that July Frank T. Fuller (September 25, 1826 - February 19, 1915), a dentist from Portsmouth, New Hampshire who was active in Republican politics and had given an oration at the 4th of July celebration at Exeter, and had been the person who suggested Bob read the *Declaration of Independence,* visited the Lincolns'. Bob had answered, "I'll do it if father is willing." So, Fuller sent a telegram to Lincoln and Abe replied, "Tell Bob to read that immortal document every chance he has, and the bigger the crowd, the louder he must holler." Fuller visited Lincoln at the State House most likely on July 19[th.] Fuller mentioned in an interview years later that there was an artist (Thomas Murphy Johnston 1836 - February 18, 1869) present whom Lincoln was in discussion with about painting his portrait and it is documented that Johnston was there on that date. After a friendly conversation, Lincoln invited Fuller home for dinner. He seemed a very nice fellow. He brought along a poster announcing the 4th of July festival that was held at Exeter and at which Bob had read the *Declaration of Independence.* The boys crawled over Frank and were very interested in his repeating watch that they had never seen before, nor had Lincoln. Frank also gave Mary a collection of poems (*Poems* published in 1859) by the Portsmouth poet Albert Laighton (June, 8, 1829 - February 6, 1887) knowing both Mary and Abe loved poetry as Willie did too. Willie thought the poems were very good, although he didn't understand some of them due to the big words. On October 20, 1861 Lincoln congratulated then Acting Governor of the Utah Territory, Frank Fuller, on completion of the telegraph line to Salt Lake City, thus uniting the Atlantic and Pacific Oceans

As the election drew near, Willie and Tad's excitement grew by leaps and bounds. In August, great parades marched down 8th Street past the Lincoln home with music, banners, posters, floats and flag waving. There were six-thousand people in one parade and it took two and one-half hours to pass. Willie and Tad watched the spectacle with shining eyes. It was like a big colorful dream.

There was also a great gathering at the Grove outside of town that ran over into the surrounding fields. All the thousands of people were fed. Willie couldn't even estimate the number of beeves [cattle-roast beef] roasted whole in the barbecue style. Deep pits looking like fresh-made graves were half-filled with wood fires and over each was suspended the carcass of a beeve that was kept turning slowly. There seemed to be miles of tables made of rough boards. The mere number of loaves of bread for the hungry multitude was a huge task for the scores of men. At intervals about the grounds were hogsheads of ice-water and wash-tubs of lemonade. At great intervals were speaker's stands at which orators spouted patriotism with grateful interruptions from brass bands and glee clubs. Willie would have liked to get up on one of those stands and give a rousing speech like his father but was afraid no one would be able to hear his small voice over the din. Anyhow, Willie had enough trouble keeping track of Tad who tended to wander off in the crowd. Even in town wigwams were erected everywhere. [These were temporary circular buildings where speeches continued into the night].

In September, Col. Elmer E. Ellsworth, who back in August thrilled Willie and Tad with his Zouave soldier drills, came to Springfield [between September 16 and 22] at Lincoln's invitation to study law with Mr. Herndon (William Henry Herndon December 25, 1819 - March 18, 1891) in Lincoln's law office. Willie and Tad were very excited to see him again. Ellsworth was short not exceeding 5'6" tall, and had a boyish figure, well-formed shapely limbs, well-balanced head crowned with dark hair that fell in careless clinging curls about his neck, eyes of dark hazel that sparkled and flashed with excitement or melted with tenderness. Delie Wheelock and Julie Sprigg (Julia [Sprigg] Wilson July 31, 1851 - March 18, 1929) swooned over him. He had organized the famous Zouaves known all around the country and they enthusiastically helped Lincoln with his campaign. The Lincolns took Ellsworth in as a member of their family. With his good looks, energy, excitement and affectionate nature not to mention his colorful uniform, Willie, Tad and all their friends fell in love with Ellsworth. All the boys wanted to be famous Zouaves. Adoringly, Willie and Tad climbed all over him when he came to visit and he loved it. Add to all that was said about Ellsworth a chivalrous personality that created a feeling of well-being, enthusiasm and gaiety in those he touched; put this romantic figure in a dashing uniform, red cap, red shirt, grey breeches, grey jacket and in his belt a sword, a heavy revolver and an enormously large Bowie knife more than a foot long. Willie admired that sword so much Abe [after Willie begged for it] got him an old sword so that Willie could be just like Elmer. Willie was rarely seen without it.

Elmer Ephraim Ellsworth was born in Malta, New York, son of Ephraim Daniel Ellsworth (May 22, 1809 - November 6, 1889) and Phoebe Denton (January 5, 1810 - March 20, 1889). Ephraim's father was George Ellsworth (1756? - March 28, 1840) who joined the Continental Army at age fifteen and fought at Saratoga and was present at Yorktown for the surrender of the British.

In Chicago in 1858 at age twenty Ellsworth met Dr. Charles A. Devilliers (1812 - 1893), a fencing instructor who had served in the French Zouave Regiment in the Crimean War and was familiar with their drills and equipment. The name and tactics were taken from a mountain tribe of Algerians (Arabic *zwawa)* in 1830.

Ellswoth became very interested in the Zouave drills and tactics and after a period of study and practice with Dr. Devilliers, adapted them to his New York firemen eventually becoming famous and known initially as the Firemen Zouaves then New York Zouaves and put on drill and acrobatic demonstrations in many cities.

Later in 1858 while drilling in Rockford, Illinois, he met Miss Carrie Spafford (Carrie [Spafford] Brett) December 2, 1842 - October 8, 1911) with whom he became engaged. Ellsworth did not drink liquor, coffee, tea and did not smoke and was above all a moral champion who insisted on the same standards with his Zouaves. On May 7, 1861, now Colonel Ellsworth, was mustered in as head of the 11th New York Volunteer Infantry.

One day late in the summer of 1860 Mr. Joseph Medill (April, 6, 1823 - March 16, 1899) called at the State House to see Lincoln and found the large room empty of visitors which was unusual ever since Abe had been nominated for president. Mr. Medill found Willie, Tad and Abe on the floor. He had just finished winding the string on the boys' top in a way that would give it the greatest force when it whirled off the floor. Lincoln looked at Mr, Medill who was grinning and explained, "I'm having a season of relaxation with my boys before the election." Abe always tried to find time in his busy schedule to play with Willie and Tad and keep life normal as possible. Willie loved him dearly for that. Some people in Springfield, especially Mr. Herndon and Mr. Lamon (Ward Hill Lamon January 6, 1828 - May 7, 1893), thought Lincoln was too lenient with the boys and let them get away with too many pranks and he should discipline them. But Willie and Tad never hurt anyone and it was all in fun and often the boys did things [they did get carried away sometimes] because they knew that Lincoln enjoyed them too. He was their father but in some ways he was like a big kid. Abe would let them do pretty much whatever they wanted [and Mary most of the time] because of both Lincoln and Mary's strict childhoods and likely physical abuse by Abe's father. Everyone knew the rail-splitter tales about Lincoln when he was growing up in Kentucky but when he was younger, about the same age as Willie was in 1860, he had great sadness in his life. His little brother Thomas "Tommy" Lincoln (1811 -1812/13) died when Abe was three or four, a sister (Sarah [Lincoln] Grigsby February 10, 1807 - January 28, 1828) and finally his mother (Nancy [Hanks] Lincoln February 5, 1784 - October 5, 1818). Mary also grew up in Kentucky but in a town, Lexington. She was from a big family and didn't get the love and attention she would have received and wanted the boys to know and feel they were loved and agreed with Abe that Willie and Tad should be able to do whatever they want as long as they didn't hurt anyone. What saved Lincoln from becoming mean and bitter like his father was the loving, kind influence his stepmother (Sarah [Bush] Lincoln December 13, 1788 - April 12, 1869) had on him growing up. She spent a lot of time with him to Abe's father's chagrin. His father was not big on "book learning" but did pay to send Abe to school for three or four years. Sarah made sure Abe learned to read and write and love books and poetry just like Abe and Mary did for Willie and Tad.

On October 7th, 1860 Colonel Elmer Ellsworth came to visit Lincoln. As usual Willie and Tad made a great fuss over him, crawling all over him.

On October 19th Lincoln replied to a little girl in New York state who wanted him to grow whiskers because she thought he'd look better. Willie and Tad weren't sure he should but Abe said, "She might have a point about me looking better with a beard." So he grew one and the boys got used to it. Willie believed that Abe thought he was ugly and that the beard would make him less so but Willie always thought he was handsome. The boys raveled out black sock yarn and pasted it and tied it all over their faces for whiskers so they could be like their father.

On November 6th the big day arrived, the election. All that day Willie and Tad anxiously awaited the news and finally that evening it was announced that Lincoln had won. Their father was the 16th president of the United States! Willie knew all along he would win. A wild night of celebration followed the announcement. The whole town seemed to come out with bands and parades that night. Willie and Tad were used to all the excitement by now and took it in stride. They fell asleep.

Thanksgiving was on November 29th that year. The family attended church at First Presbyterian in the morning and had their big roast turkey dinner in the afternoon. Willie and the family were very thankful that Abe had been elected president.

On December 21st, his 10th birthday, Willie had his last party in Springfield. Mary had invited twenty or thirty boys and girls and it was a fine time but sad also because Willie knew he would be leaving his friends in a month or so not knowing for sure if or when he'd ever be back.

Willie's brother Bob had started college at Harvard that September and Willie got a chance to practice his letter writing. Willie loved to write letters, little speeches, and little sermons and was going to try to write poems someday soon.

Bob returned home for Christmas and the family had a joyous family reunion. Willie and Tad's stockings that hung at the fireplace were unusually full of candy, fruit and small toys that year and Willie suspected that Bob had helped St. Nicholas out and snuck some extra goodies in the stockings after St. Nicholas left.

January 1861 was a hectic time. Preparations for the Lincolns' move to Washington began. Lincoln made arrangements for the house Willie had lived in for ten years and the family for seventeen to be rented out. They had to find homes for their pets too. Willie and Tad did not want to leave Fido and begged their father to let them take him with them. The boys loved Fido dearly. Abe decided not to take Fido to Washington because he was terrified of clanging church bells, cannons and other loud noises such as the train whistle, and engine noises would scare him. Abe believed Fido would not survive the long train ride. Willie and Tad pestered and begged but this was one time Lincoln would not give in and it was settled that the John E. Roll (John Eddy Roll June 9, 1814 - March 30, 1901) family who had two boys, John (John Linden Roll June 25, 1854 - November 13, 1943) and Frank (Frank Pelmer Roll March 5, 1852 - February 26, 1939) who were about Willie and Tad's ages would take care of Fido who always liked them. In the end Willie knew his father was right. It would not have been fair to put Fido through the long ordeal of a train ride. To assure the boys that Fido would be well-treated Lincoln asked the Roll family to never scold him for coming in the house with muddy paws. He was not to be tied-up alone in the backyard. He was to be allowed in the Roll house whenever he scratched at the front door and into the dining room at mealtimes. Fido was used to being given table scraps by the family. To make Fido feel more at home at the Rolls'. Abe gave them the Lincolns' horsehair sofa that Fido loved to sleep on. When Mr. Roll came for Fido the boys cried and hugged him and said their goodbyes. Willie felt bad for his father, too, as he couldn't take his favorite horse Old Bob. In April of 1865 the Rolls' took *Fido to F. W. Ingmire's Studio, opened in 1862 (Frederick William Ingmire (September 11, 1822 - September 20, 1876) to have his picture taken. Mr. Ingmire draped a piece of fancy material over a wash stand and placed Fido on top. Fido looked patient in the photograph as if to do whatever was required of him. Sadly, Fido had a tragic ending. Sometime in 1866 he was accidentally stabbed by one Charles Planck (December 10, 1842 - March 21, 1917) a Civil War veteran, and son of Springfield grocer Jacob C. Planck (June 27, 1804 - August 2, 1867). Planck, who allegedly had been drinking, was whittling a piece of wood when Fido came bounding along and, as usual, sprang forward with his forepaws raised in his way of greeting and Planck, (possibly suffering from a PTSD* reflex action) stabbed poor Fido in the chest. Poor Fido, wounded, weakened and bleeding profusely, struggled to make it home to the Roll house but it was too far. He made it to the rear of the old Universalist Church at fifth and Cook, curled up against the chimney and died. It was several days before Fido's body was discovered. The Roll boys carried him home and poor old Fido was buried in the backyard of the Roll house at 2nd and Cook, a spot that is kept sacred to this day.

*Planck had served from 1862-65 as a corporal in Company G, 114th Illinois Volunteer Regiment and fought in several battles.

*Perhaps Preston Butler (1818 -?), who is listed in the *1860 Springfield City Directory* as having a "photographic & ambrotype gallery on the square" took a photo of Fido that is lost. He took the one of Mary, Willie and Tad and maybe the one of Eddy and probably the earlier ones of Willie, and the ambrotypes of Willie with a lock of his hair.

On February 7th, 1861 Willie and his family left their house and moved for a few days to the Chenery House. This hotel had new gas-lighting jets and Willie didn't know that he wasn't supposed to blow them out and he did. Abe told Willie that he must not do that. Willie said that his mother let him blow out the lamps [oil] at home. Lincoln explained that these new gas jets were for lighting that stays on all the time. Willie learned something that day.

On the morning of February 8th Lincoln received a package from Mr. A. P. Russell, (Addison Peale Russell September 8, 1826 - July 24, 1912) Secretary of State of Ohio that contained an unusual gift. It was a whistle made out of a pig's tail. Lincoln laughed and tried to play it and was surprised it actually made music, sort of. He said, "I never suspected up to this time that there was music in such a thing as that." Then, before Willie had a chance to try, Tad grabbed it and generally made a nuisance of himself all day "playing" it and "hogging" it.

Journey to Washington
February 11 - February 23, 1861

On the morning of February 11th Lincoln and Bob left on the *train to the cheers of the large crowd even though it was raining. Standing at the rear of the last car Lincoln gave his farewell to Springfield speech he had read to the family the night before and they all loved it but Willie thought to himself it was kinda' sad.

"My friends…No one, not in my situation, can appreciate my feeling of sadness at this parting. To this place and the kindness of these people, I owe everything…I now leave, …with a task before me greater than that which rested upon Washington…Trusting in Him, who can go with me, and can remain with you…I bid you an affectionate farewell."

Mary, Willie and Tad left on the train that same evening to catch-up with Abe in Indianapolis. Mary and the boys wanted to surprise Abe for his 52nd birthday February 12th. They originally weren't supposed to join Lincoln till later in Washington. Lincoln didn't look too surprised when they all met in Indianapolis. Willie suspected someone told him they were on the later train. The Presidential Car was decorated with flags and red, white and blue festoons hung from the moldings. The walls were covered with crimson plush and heavy blue silk studded with silver stars, smoke trailing behind in great plumes. For Willie it was the most exciting journey of his young life since the trip he and his father had taken by train to Chicago in June 1859. Willie delighted his father by keeping a timetable and noting the exact moment of every stop and departure. Willie and Tad ran from car to car playing hide and seek making a nuisance of themselves to the astonished passengers. Tad got the idea he and Willie should play tricks on the people at the stops along the way who were always clambering, "Show us tall Abe!" "Show us the railsplitter!" "You want to see old Abe?" The boys would holler back. "Well, *there* he is!" And then they'd point out Judge David Davis (March 9, 1815 - June 26, 1886) or Ward Lamon who didn't look anything like their father.

*A special Great Western Railroad train.

At the stopover in New York the boys' nursemaid took them to see a play at Laura Keene's (Laura Keene July 20, 1826 - November 4, 1873) Theatre and with Abe and Mary to see Barnum's Museum that reminded the boys of the Niagara Falls Museum they saw in 1857 but bigger with many more weird curiosities and mammoth monstrosities. New York was even larger than Chicago and more crowded with people.

They arrived in Harrisburg, the capital of Pennsylvania on Washington's birthday February 22nd about 1:30 in the afternoon. They had to walk in the rain the three blocks from the station to their hotel. Lincoln had to make a speech at the State House so Mary, Willie and Tad stayed indoors in their suite at the *Jones House Hotel on Market Square. Although Mary tried to keep it from the boys, they found out that due to a threat on their father's life he had to take a different route to Washington that night leaving about midnight. Mary was very worried but Willie tried to calm her saying, "No one can hurt father!" And he believed it.

*This is now a bank and the city bus transfer center is right across from it. I walk those same three blocks (with deja vu feelings) several times a week that Mary and the boys walked that rainy day, February

22, 1861, that coincidentally is the same day, also rainy, February 22, 2018, I write this.

As much as Willie was excited about his father becoming president and the move to Washington, he had mixed feelings about it. He was going to a new place, unknown, and not sure what to expect. Willie had even *deeper* feelings, sort of like a bad dream that won't go away right away in the morning when you first wake-up but holds you in an emotional residue of fear and anxiety. He had a sense of foreboding and sadness but not sure why.

WASHINGTON

FEBRUARY 23, 1861 - FEBRUARY 20, 1862

MARY, WILLIE AND Tad arrived in Washington at the B & O Station on the morning of February 23rd and were taken to Willard's Hotel, suite six, where they were to stay until the move to the Executive Mansion [name used for White House at that time] at 1600 Pennsylvania Avenue. On the way to Willard's they saw the Capitol building still unfinished and other impressive buildings, the General Post Office, Treasury and Smithsonian Institution and off in the distance the unfinished spire of the Washington Monument. The streets were crowded with lots of people and soldiers. Another thing Willie noticed right away was the faint, foul odor, not just the usual odor of animal dung, but something else. Willie asked his father what it was. "That's from the Potomac River and the connecting canal. I'm told people throw everything in it. They say the smell is much worse in hot weather so I guess we will just have to get used to it." Willie replied, "It's sure not clean like home, is it father?" Abe just winked at his son.

Willard's was crowded with people taking papers back and forth to Lincoln and having meetings with him. Willie and Tad roamed the halls exploring the place.

On March 4th, Abraham Lincoln was inaugurated the 16th president of the United States. The largest crowd Willie ever saw awaited him and his family in front of the Capitol. After Lincoln gave his inaugural address, the Lincolns were driven to the big white house, the Executive Mansion, where they were to live for the next four years. As they were going in the door of the Mansion many people followed them in and stared at Willie and Tad. Willie couldn't understand it and said out loud, "I wish they wouldn't stare at us. Wasn't there ever a president who had children?"

The next day Willie and Tad explored every nook and cranny of the huge building. There were so many rooms, closets, attic, garret, ladder to the roof, they lost count at thirty-one rooms. They couldn't help thinking what a swell place to make up pranks to make their father laugh. The boys wanted to explore the grounds outside but it was too windy and cold. That night Mary Lincoln made her famous warm currant-vanilla cake. Actually, she made two cakes. One for Willie and Tad and one for the adults to which she added her "special" ingredient, brandy. The cake made Willie and Tad feel like it was more like home.

Tad called the old doorkeeper of the Mansion "Goatie" because of his gray and white goatee. While the boys were exploring the Mansion they found the elevator and Tad said he would ride it up and down and never get caught. Willie told Tad Goatie won't allow it but said as he often did, "Pa is president and we are his sons. We can do anything we want!" Willie told him that their mother would be real mad and that they can't just do *anything* they want. Willie added that their mother is afraid that we'd bung-up the gold piano or something. Tad countered saying they could play hide and seek and play tricks like they did at home. Willie agreed but was worried Tad would get carried away.

Aunt Lizzie Edwards (Elizabeth Porter [Todd] Edwards November 13, 1813 - February 22, 1888) intercepted the boys and took them to the family room for a belated meal. Tad asked her if the whole house was theirs. Willie thought that was a dumb question and told Tad that of course it was while their father was president. Aunt Lizzie said that she was overwhelmed that her own sister, their mother, was living in it and how it was a great privilege for the boys to be living in it. Tad asked why. Again, Willie thought it was obvious why…because of the great history associated with it, all the presidents and their families who had lived there over the years and what boy doesn't dream of being president and living there. Lizzie noted too that many famous people had visited there. Willie asked if kings had but she said she didn't know about that.

Lizzie said that their mother had asked her to tell the boys to never venture outside the main gate of the Mansion alone and Tad thought it was because she was worried they'd get lost. Willie explained that there were rebs and seceshes [secessionists] who might want to kidnap or hurt them since they were the president's sons. Lizzie didn't want Willie to continue explaining but he assured her he already knew there were some people who didn't like their father and he knew about the bad letters his father had received back home in Springfield and both boys had seen the cartoons about Lincoln in the papers that made fun of him…one with feathers and stuff. Lizzie misunderstood when Willie and Tad laughed about it thinking they were being disrespectful. She didn't know that Abe laughed about the cartoons too.

The second floor of the Mansion was the Lincoln family's living quarters. A room in the shape of an oval Lincoln made into the family's private parlor and library with its dark bookcases placed against the walls. Lincoln's office adjoined the library. The library became Willie's favorite place to sit and study and read and write. Down the hall was Willie and Tad's bedroom and another room next to it for guests. At the east end were the offices of Mr. Hay (John Milton Hay October 8, 1838 - July 1, 1905) and Mr. Nicolay (John George Nicolay February 26, 1832 - September 26, 1901), Lincoln's secretaries, and the office waiting room. Abe and Mary's bedroom was across the hall from the boys'. The northwest corner had a bedroom that served as the State Bedroom. It had a dressing room on the corner and a bedchamber named "The Prince of Wales" in honor of the prince (Prince Albert Edward November 9, 1841 - May 6, 1910) who had stayed there during the administration of President James Buchanan (April 23, 1791 - June 1, 1868). Running down the center was the hall used only as a passageway to the various offices and bedrooms. It was cold and drafty but Willie and Tad enjoyed running full speed up and down its length. The boys also enjoyed not having to go to an outhouse as there was a W.C. [water closet].

One of the first new pranks the boys played was when they saw a group of grave, bearded gentlemen assembling downstairs. Although they didn't know it at the time it was the first meeting of Lincoln's cabinet. The boys got out their toy cannon with plenty of rounds of caps and bombarded the meeting. Lincoln, grinning, stopped the meeting and said that maybe the boys should take that [the cannon] outside.

It didn't take long for Willie and Tad to get under the skin of Ward Lamon, Lincoln's sometime body guard [although Willie didn't think his father needed one as his father could take care of himself] and long-time friend, and under the skin of John Nicolay and John Hay with their pranks. A couple of times the boys were playing tag and running in and out of Lincoln's office and Lamon scooped them up and carried them out to their loud protests. John Hay also chased Willie out of the office one time. Willie was scared and yelled, "Mother!" The boys were called "hellcats" but Abe would not let Lamon, Nicolay or Hay do anything to them. Willie knew that he and Tad wouldn't have gotten away with half the stuff they did if Abe hadn't laughed and thought them "smart" [19th century use meaning humorously clever].

On Friday, March 8th, 1861 the first big levee [dinner party] was held that evening in the Mansion. Mary Lincoln wore her bright rose-colored, moiré-antique dress that her Mantua-maker Mrs. Keckly (Elizabeth Hobbs Keckly February 1818 - May 26, 1907) had sewn for her. Mrs. Keckly was a very nice mulatto lady. All the ladies wore elegant dresses and Abe shook so many hands that his got swollen. Willie and Tad ran among the throng talking to some of the officers in their bright blue uniforms. Willie ate too many chocolate bonbons and his stomach hurt.

On Sunday, March 10th, Willie, who had taken music lessons back in Springfield, went into the Red Room after lunch and sat down at the piano and started to play popular *aires* (songs) such as *Old Dog Tray, Home Sweet Home* and *My Old Kentucky Home*. Cousin Lizzie (Elizabeth Todd [Grimsley] Jacoby) May 10, 1838 - October 2, 1878), came into the room and reproved him at the first opportunity saying, "No one is without example, and as your father's son you should remember the Sabbath and keep it holy." Willie solemnly promised to never play the piano on the Sabbath again and he kept his word. Thereafter when the rest of the family went on a Sunday afternoon carriage drive, Willie stayed home with Lizzie and went to the library where it was very peaceful and read or wrote. This was a big change from back in Springfield where the boys could do whatever they wanted on Sunday but Willie understood it was better to be respectful on the Sabbath.

On Tuesday, March 12th, Willie and Tad were watching the goldfish in the Water Lily Tank in the Conservatory that joined the Executive Mansion on the west side when looking up they saw three boys [they had no friends in Washington] about their ages and a small, pretty girl who turned out to be sixteen but looked twelve. They were the children of Horatio Nelson Taft, Sr. (January 13, 1806 - April 15, 1888) and Mary Malvina (Cook) Taft (July 30, 1812 - April 5, 1905); Julia "Julie" (Taft) Bayne (March 8, 1845 - December 14, 1933), Horatio Nelson Taft, Jr. (January 15, 1847 - January 6, 1915), who was known as "Bud," was Willie's height but turned out to be fourteen. Halsey Cook Taft (August 17, 1849 - September 28, 1897) known as "Holly," was eleven and was Tad's size and little William "Willie" Taft (October 30, 1853 - September 27, 1926) was seven. Mr. Taft, known as "Judge," who worked in the Patent Office, was a friend of Lincoln's and he and Mary knowing the boys missed their friends back in Springfield arranged the meeting. Willie especially missed Henry Remann and Edward John McClernand (December 29, 1848 - February 9, 1926) and had no one to play with cooped up in the Mansion. The Taft's lived near Franklin Square on L-Street a short walk for Willie and Tad. They all soon became great friends and had a great time running around the Mansion. Bud became Willie's best friend. Bud reminded Willie of Henry in that he also liked to read a lot and was more thoughtful than Tad and Holly who were kind of wild at times. Willie and Bud didn't always participate in Tad and Holly's most outrageous pranks. Willie and Bud had a special, intuitive understanding of each other. It was like they could read each other's minds and knew what the other was thinking and going to say before he said it. Abe also took a great liking to Bud. Willie Taft often tagged along after Tad and Holly and got caught up in their pranks.

Although Bud was four years older than Willie, they were about the same height. The Taft boys were small in stature. Bud was pale and languid like Willie, soft-spoken and loved to read and was a pretty good scholar like Willie. Holly made a great comrade for Tad as he was all motion and activity, never idle, impatient of restraint, quick to learn when he tried, impetuous, all "go-ahead;" characteristics he shared with Tad. Little Willie Taft had dark hair and eyes, was a ceaseless talker, ambitious to know everything, always asking questions, always busy, never sitting still like Bud and Willie. Tad, Holly and Willie Taft are much alike in disposition.

Early the next morning, March 13th, one of the gardeners escorted Willie and Tad over to the Taft's where they stayed and played till evening. That evening Willie asked his father if he and Tad could go alone to the Taft's since they now knew the way and Abe said fine.

Willie had discovered the center of the Mansion's bell system in the garret. Tad figured out how to work the bells and although Willie told Tad not to do it, he had the whole place in bedlam. It was great fun although Hay and Nicolay didn't think it funny and called the boys hell-cats. The boys didn't realize that the bells were an alert that the rebels were invading and had soldiers, servants and everyone scurrying around the Mansion looking for the enemy. That night after supper Lincoln took the boys aside and said, "That was pretty funny boys, you'll likely to give Hay and Nicolay heart attacks," and they all laughed, even Mary, who wasn't too fond of either gentleman.

Although Tad didn't like Goatie as he called the old doorkeeper Edward McManus (1818 - June 7, 1890), Willie made friends with him. For some reason Tad either really liked someone or really didn't, a personality trait he shared with his mother. Abe told Tad the world wasn't black and white and most people are not all good or all bad and he should try to overlook some of the bad and see more of the good. Willie was not sure that Tad understood what their father meant but hoped he would when he was older. Mr. McManus was nice enough to take time out from his doorman's duties to act as Willie's train dispatcher. The office seekers who poured into the Mansion were the trains. Some knew where they were going. They were the expresses. Those who inquired were the locals and Willie directed them to their proper tracks. Some of the office seekers were so stupid and clumsy that they got derailed and wandered about till their momentum died down. There were long lines of freights on settee sidings before the presidential office door.

Lincoln had given Willie and Tad pocket knives and they carved a "war map" on top of a table in the northeast room upstairs. Tad got real mad and try to make a war map out of Willie. Willie did something with his pocket knife that he later felt bad about. Mr. Hay was always calling the boys hell-cats that which made Willie mad and he snuck into Hay's office and cut into ribbons the cloth covering his writing table. Abe probably wished he'd never given the boys knives but said nothing about it.

Willie and Tad came down with measles and had to postpone playing with the Taft boys for two weeks. Cousin Lizzie Grimsley, who was visiting from Kentucky, nursed them. Unfortunately, the boys gave the measles to Elmer Ellsworth who was visiting…a bad case, too. Willie and Tad always climbed all over him when he came which he loved and that's how he contracted it. Willie felt really bad that they had gotten him sick because Willie feared Elmer would no longer be with them drilling, playing games and wrestling with the war talk everywhere. Willie was so very proud of him but worried that something might happen to him. Ellsworth had promised to teach them *The Manual of Arms* before he left.

Dr. Robert King Stone (December 11, 1822 - April 23, 1872), who was the Lincoln family doctor in Washington, came to the Mansion to treat the boys. After he explained that the measles were very contagious, that confirmed that the boys had given it to Elmer. Willie said to the doctor, "I wish Mr. Stanton (Edwin McMasters Stanton December 19, 1814 - December 24, 1869), who was advisor to the Secretary of War, Simon Cameron (March 8, 1799 - June 26, 1889), would come in here." Willie never liked Stanton as he was mean to him and Tad and never had time for them, and Willie wished Stanton had caught the measles instead of Elmer.

The boys missed the snows of "yesteryear" in Springfield., so, along with Bud and Holly, made pretend-snow in the attic out of a large bin of old visiting cards. To play snowstorm they made a sled out of an old chair minus a seat, nailed barrel stoves to it for runners and used an old copy of the *Congressional Record* for a seat. They dragged it around through the "snow" throwing the cards up in the air and stuffed them down each other's backs like they did with real snow in Springfield.

Willie and Tad went to see the Flying Artillery that were exercising at Franklin Square where they met their new friends, Julia, Bud, Holly and Willie Taft.

Willie was devoted to Tad but he had to be careful what he said to him. He was very sensitive and would cry or get mad at the slightest thing. Willie always tried to cheer him up. One morning at breakfast Tad was really upset and couldn't, or wouldn't stop crying because some soldiers he had tried to give religious tracts to had laughed at him. Lincoln couldn't even bring him out of it and looked over at Willie. Willie was concentrating on what to say to Tad and finally clasped his hands together, shut his teeth over his lower lip and looked up into his father's face. Abe knew Willie knew what to say and exclaimed, "There!

You have it now my boy, have you not?" Lincoln then turned to a guest who was at the breakfast table with them and said, "I know every step of the process by which that boy arrived at his satisfactory solution of the question before him and it's by such slow methods I attain results." Willie said, "Tad, listen to me. The soldiers that laughed at you when you tried to bring them the word of God were just ignorant. Don't let those few fellows discourage you. Why, I bet there's a whole slew of others who would be glad to have the comfort of the message in those tracts. Tad stopped crying, looked up at Willie and said, "You're right Willie. I'll try some again after breakfast."

Easter Sunday, March 31st was a chilly morning. Willie and Tad had been going to church [Fourth Street Presbyterian] with the Taft's however Julie was unwell and didn't go.

Monday, April 1st was the day of the egg-rolling on the Executive Mansion's grounds and Willie and Tad couldn't wait. The evening before Abe and Mary had helped the boys color a basket of eggs for the occasion. The boys were up and out early. Bud, Holly, little Willie and Julie came too. At the rear of the Mansion was a sloping lawn with soft turf. All the children which included Willie and Tad's friends, those from the neighborhood, and the children of the African-American servants gathered at the top of the hill and watched their eggs in a race to the bottom. The one that arrived first without being cracked was the winner. The cracked or broken ones go to the victor who eats them, or at least is expected to. Willie and Tad watched in disappointment as one boy started yelling that he'd won but when his egg was examined it turned out to be made of china. The little cheat caused confusion among the judges until it was decided that first place should go to a boy named Tom who would be declared the winner. Tad was really mad and said, "I'm going to bring an iron egg next year!"

Willie and Tad went over to the Taft's to see their litter of chicks. The boys played with the little peeping things for a while.

April 11th Fort Sumpter in South Carolina was attacked by the rebels at 4:30 in the morning.

With war being declared everyone in the Mansion was running in and out, tearing up the stairs with handfuls of papers, frowning, swearing, talking, bragging and calling names. Willie ran out and bought some newspapers to see what the headlines were. *The Evening Star* had the following:

"It is at last decided that Fort Sumpter shall be reinforced. The Cabinet have issued orders for the evacuation of Fort Sumpter. Orders were sent off last evening to reinforce Major Robert Anderson (June 14, 1805 - October 17, 1871) at all costs. It is believed that Major Anderson evacuated Fort Sumpter by order of the government last evening…"

Fort Sumpter had not been reinforced but brave Major Anderson fights on with 70 men against the rebels who have 10,000 men and 19 batteries.

On Saturday, April 13th Abe, Nicolay, Willie and Tad took a carriage ride that lasted till near supper time. That evening they heard that Major Anderson evacuated the Fort and it surrendered.

Lincoln had called for 75,000 troops to defend the Union. Willie and Tad cleared a central space in the attic of the Mansion that represented Charleston Harbor. Tad sheltered behind a barricade of chairs, small table, books and other odds and ends that represented the walls of Fort Sumpter. A fleet of blocks were the relief ships sent by their father to carry food to Major Anderson's garrison. Willie manned a shore battery laying on his stomach and pounded the fort with his mortars. The shot and shell consisted of peanuts fired by rubber bands. They could hurt too. The objective was a small American flag flying from a ruler-flagstaff on Fort Sumpter. Tad had said Willie was to be the rebs. Willie was philosophic about it as he knew there had to be rebels if there was to be a rebellion. Willie had talked Mrs. Keckly into sewing him up a Confederate flag which she reluctantly agreed to this one time and said, "Don't ask me to soil my hands making a rebel flag again!" Willie felt ashamed he'd asked. He didn't think of Mrs. Keckly as a "negro" who would naturally be sensitive about sewing a rebel flag. Willie thought of her as an aunt who was very kind to him and Tad and often read to them. Willie tried to smooth things over by stating firmly, "Father had called for 75,000 troops. They'll see that the rebs get licked.!" Mrs. Keckly shook her head. "It's going to take a sight more troops than that, boy. I've been down south and I know. They're rich and they're proud and there's millions of them." Mrs. Keckly added with pride that her son George (George "William H." Kirkland January 1842 - August 10, 1861 [killed in battle]) a free man, had joined up to fight the rebs. He was in Company D of the 1st Regiment of Missouri Infantry. Willie was moved. Suddenly the war had come very close. Little did Willie know that George would be killed four months later.

Colonel Ellsworth would soon be in it too but Willie thought *he will be alright* he prayed. No one so brave and dashing as a Zouave colonel *could be hurt*. Willie was worried about Mrs. Keckly's son whom he'd never met. As he lay on his stomach firing cannon at Fort Sumpter he thought about him. Tad mocked Willie's misses. But at length the Union flag was hit. "Surrender! Surrender! You're Smashed!" Willie yelled. But Major Anderson was having too much fun to surrender. "You've got to surrender." Willie said, stopping the bombardment to rub his eye. "Your food is gone. Your garrison is stifled by hear and smoke. Your relief ships will never get to you, and you've been under bombardment for 33 hours. You've got to surrender." "I won't!" Tad cried. There was but one answer. More war. Willie charged across Charleston Harbor, wrecked the front of Sumpter, threw Major Anderson down and began to grind his scalp with his knuckles. "Will you surrender now?" Tad wriggled free of Willie but he was too light to beat Willie in a frontal attack, but he was quicker. Tad ran downstairs half with excitement, half with laughter and plunged for protection into their father's study.

April 19th the 6th Massachusetts Infantry Regiment was attacked by secesch in Baltimore on their way to Washington. Approximately four soldiers and nine citizens were killed.

The next day when the Massachusetts Regiment arrived in Washington everybody cheered them as they marched down Pennsylvania Avenue.

On Sunday, the Lincoln family gathered on the portico of the Mansion as the 7th Regimental Band played gloriously on the shaven lawn at the south front of the Mansion. The scene was very beautiful. The gaily dressed strolled idly. Soldiers loafed in the promenades. The martial music of soul-stirring national aires filled the sweet air with suggestions of heroism.

The next day, April 22nd, Willie and Tad's Uncle, Captain Lockwood Marcus Todd (1823 - January 9, 1894), came to visit and wanted photographs of the boys so he took them to Matthew Brady's Studio to pose with him. Tad had trouble sitting still for the exposure so he sat in a chair while Willie stood next to their Uncle who was also seated. It turned out to be a fine photograph. Captain had his walking stick with him so Willie asked if he could have a photograph of him standing with it. This was the best likeness of Willie Lincoln and the last known photograph of him. Tad also had his photograph taken with the walking stick.

On April 23rd the powerful warship the Pawnee arrived on the Potomac.

April 24th six-hundred Kansas Volunteers camped in the East Room. They came to replace the Clay Battalion to guard the Mansion. Willie, Tad, Bud and Holly got cookies from the kitchen and took them to the soldiers. The boys spent a lot of time learning how to disassemble and clean rifles and how to cook on camp fires on the lawn. The soldiers told the boys tales of their battles against secesch in Kansas. The Kansas Volunteers had taken the place of the Clay Battalion that was hastily organized by Lincoln's friend Cassius Marcellus Clay (October 10, 1810 - July 23, 1903), the abolitionist from Kentucky. It consisted mostly of civilians, retired military men and others who were to guard the Mansion until regular troops from the north arrived. Bud's father, Horatio Nelson Taft, Sr., was a member of the Clay Battalion.

Willie and Tad watched a huge review of troops, the 7th New York, and troops from Massachusetts and Rhode Island march by the

Mansion bands playing and banners unfurled. Willie watched from the front gate proudly holding the sword that his father had given him that looked like Col. Elmer Ellsworth's.

Willie, Tad and the Taft boys soon got caught up in the ardent patriotism watching the regiments that marched in review down Pennsylvania Avenue and visiting the military camps with Abe and Mary. The boys had Union badges adorning their jackets, played more war-oriented games and had war-oriented toys. They had guns, [inoperable of course] swords and miniature Union uniforms. To the boys' beloved Colonel Elmer Ellsworth, war meant longingly and darkly more than any of these things.

On April 27, Willie and Tad went over to the Taft's to play with Bud, Holly and little Willie about 10 o'clock. On the way they passed more and more camps of the newly arriving soldiers. Willie thought that the city now seems like one big camp [the city's population had grown from a pre-war 30,000 to 100,000 with the constant influx of troops in 1861].

The next day workmen came and installed marble-topped washstands with fancy painted porcelain sinks in the Mansion family bedrooms. Each had a single hydrant that when turned parallel to the wall was off and when swung out over the bowl flowed with cold Potomac River water for washing [big sanitary mistake]. Crisp linen towels were put daily at the stands. Mary warned the boys NOT to drink from the washstand water as it was not safe. A pitcher of spring water were placed on the boys' bed stand for drinking. The boys were supposed to only drink from the spigots in the first floor kitchen or servant level below the kitchen as that spring water came from the well at Franklin Square. But sometimes, if it was a cold night and their water pitcher was empty and they didn't feel like running down stairs in their bare feet and nightshirts, they may have drunk a little from the washstand although it tasted funny.

The Rhode Island Regiment came and was reviewed by General Winfield Scott (June 13, 1786 - May 29, 1866), and the Cabinet. Mr.

and Mrs. Taft, Julia and little Willie Taft were in the East Room. Willie and Tad were out riding till the review was nearly over.

April 30th three Indians from the Potowatomi Tribe, one a giant wearing a bear-claw necklace, called on their Great Father in the Mansion.

Spring had arrived in Washington and the trees and flowers, particularly the bed of red and white camellias that Mary Lincoln had the gardener plant, were blooming.

May 3rd Willie wrote to Henry Remann in Springfield. He hadn't written to him since he left back in February. Willie told him about all the soldiers [ten thousand] stationed at the Capitol building and about the Lincolns' dear friend Colonel Elmer Ellsworth going to New York to organize a regiment that he brought to Washington the day before. He told Henry that they had special bright-colored uniforms and because they were acrobatic and helped fight fires they were called the "firemen" by some people but their real names were the Zouaves.

The Lincolns went to see Ellsworth's Zouave firemen regimental swearing-in at the east front of the Capitol where they were named the 11th New York Regiment. Ellsworth then formed them in a hollow square and made a great, rousing, patriotic speech. His men all yelled, "Bully for you!":

Ellsworth's Zouaves paraded daily past the Executive Mansion and he always waved when he saw Willie and Tad.

On May 9th Willard's Hotel caught on fire but after a two-hour struggle, Ellsworth's brave and skillful Zouaves, two standing on the roof which was engulfed in flames, each holding the leg of a comrade dangling over the edge to reach the hose, finally succeeded in squelching the inferno and saving the building.

That afternoon the 71st New York Regimental Band performed a concert at the Navy Yard. After the concert Lincoln and the boys went aboard the steamer the U.S.S. Pensacola and watched the cannon [11-inch Dahlgren (John Adolphus Bernard Dahlgren November 14, 1809 - July 12, 1870) gun] practice. They could see the ball shoot through the air till it hit its target out in the river with a huge splash. When they came off the ship the 71st was having a dress parade.

May 11th Lincoln held an impromptu levee for children. Willie, Tad and all their friends had a great time. Afterwards, Carl Schurz (March 2, 1829 - May 14, 1906) stayed for tea with Abe.

The boys heard that Ellsworth's regiment was moved to Fort Lincoln four miles out on the road to Alexandria. Willie was both excited and fearful that Elmer would soon be in the fight.

Mrs. Taft, Julia, Bud, Holly and little Willie all came to the Mansion to watch the Grand Review of the District Military.

May 15th Lincoln reviewed new companies of troops, 6,500 arriving at the Mansion to replace the Kansas Volunteers. Now stationed on the lawn were soldiers from New York, Massachusetts and the Pennsylvania Volunteers.

May 17th Willie visited with a soldier friend at his bivouac on the lawn till "Drum Beat" at 9:30 when all soldiers had to be in their quarters. Then Willie went to bed.

Willie heard that Julie had visited Colonel Ellsworth at his new encampment at Fort Lincoln. Willie wished that he'd been invited along but he knew all the young girls swooned over Elmer.

Lincoln liked Bud Taft a lot. He sent Bud, who was 14, on errands. Willie was a little jealous but his father reminded him Bud was older. Abe asked Bud to go out and buy him a pair of rubbers. Willie and Bud went to Abe's closet and found an old shoe (BIG) and Bud took it around town till he found the right size. Bud hadn't let on it was for the president and the clerk told Bud, "I think your father must have the largest feet [121/2 B] in Washington."

Willie and Tad spent a lot of time at the Taft's on L Street. Monsieur Jordan (1782 - ?) an old Frenchman, lived across L Street from the Taft's. He told the boys stories of his service in Napoleon's Old Guard, battles and exploits. The boys peppered him with questions. Whenever he mentioned Napoleon he would pull off his blue cap. Later Tad bragged that he made him pull it off nine times. Willie answered, "Yea, but you asked questions out of turn, Tad Lincoln, and that isn't fair." Tad had a habit of saying and doing stuff without thinking how it would affect others. Willie loved his little brother but sometimes he really made Willie and others mad. Like the time he ate all the strawberries in the garden that were meant for a state dinner. Willie told his mother what Tad had done and she wasn't too happy but simply told him to stay out of the garden in the future (like he really would, thought Willie).

Bud's older half-brother, Surgeon Charles Sabin Taft (August 1835 - December 18, 1900) took Willie, Tad, Julie and the three Taft boys to see Col. Ellsworth's special gymnastics drill at Camp Lincoln. Their skill and precision was amazing and they all clapped and shouted, "Bully!" at the conclusion. As they were leaving, Elmer stood at the corner waving his red cap smiling and calling, "Come again!"

May 24th Willie and Tad were out at the stables watching Francis Burns (1824 - December 18, 1878), the coachman, polish a harness when suddenly they heard the bells of the Mansion ringing and wondered if someone thought it was Sunday by mistake. The coachman stopped rubbing the silver and said, "Now what could they be tolling them for?" Tad stepped out of the stables to see. The Stars and Stripes on the Mansion pole were being hauled down. Tad ran back in the stables and said excitedly, "They're taking down the flag. The rebels haven't won, have they?" "Of course not!" Willie yelled at him. "Do you think father would let 'em?" Willie added, but was worried something serious had happened. The boys ran back into the Mansion looking for someone to tell them what was going on. Lincoln wasn't in his study and they found him in their parents' bedroom. Mary was lying down on a lounge crying. "Mother, what is it? Are you sick again?" Willie asked, very upset. "Do they put the flag at half-mast when mother is sick?" Tad asked. Abe was standing at the window looking out. When he turned around Willie saw that he also had been crying. Willie was then frightened for he knew whatever had happened had to be very serious for his father to cry like that. Lincoln came over to Willie and Tad and put his big, long arms around their shoulders. He said, "You boys must be brave as soldiers. Colonel Ellsworth has been taken from us" "Taken where?" Tad asked. "Did the rebels get him?" "That means he's dead." Willie said, hardly believing his own words as they sounded unreal and strange to his ears. "How, Father? How?" Willie cried, tears welling-up in his eyes. "He was murdered by the proprietor, James William Jackson of the Marshall House, a hotel over in Alexandria, as he was coming down the stairs with the rebel flag he had torn down from the roof." Then it hit Willie. All the fun they'd had with "Uncle" (they thought of him as a member of the family) Elmer; the wrestling, watching him drilling the Zouaves, he and his comrades' acrobatics, fighting fires, his, promise to teach them *The Manual of Arms*, never, never, never would happen. Willie and Tad cried and were inconsolable.

May 25th was a very sad day for all. They brought the beloved Elmer's body back to the Executive Mansion and he lay in his coffin on a bier in the East Room where thousands came to see him. Mr. and Mrs. Taft, Bud and Holly came and Willie asked where little Willie was and his father said they didn't bring him as he would be tempted to run into the crowd and get separated from the family. Julie, weeping softly, placed a wreath of white roses on Elmer's breast. Mary Lincoln placed a laurel wreath in wax encircling a picture of Elmer on the coffin. Abe looked very pale as if he was still in shock, eyes downcast. Mrs. Keckly held Willie's hand and they both wept for the half-hour it took for the weeping Zouaves to file past their fallen leader. He was only 24 years old. Later that day Willie and Tad were upstairs with their cousin Lizzie who had come to visit at the Mansion for a while and Tad asked, "They were crying, the soldiers. I didn't know they ever did that?" "They do," Mary Lincoln said coming into the room, "when they are very sad as they are now because their colonel is dead." "But you always say when I cry that soldiers don't cry like I do," Tad replied. Willie said to Tad, "You don't cry because something important has happened like you friend being shot in a war. You cry because you didn't get what you wanted." Willie asked, "Mother, what happens to Elmer now?" "Why, they'll send him home and bury him in the cemetery in Mechanicville his home town in New York." "And that's *all?*" Willie asked feeling really sad. "How could he be so *alive* and putting on that special gymnastic drill with his Zouaves this time day before yesterday and now he's all cold and white-looking and lying in a box?" Willie asked. "Everybody dies!" Tad said and ran out of the room. "That's true isn't it? We *never know* when we'll die which is really unfair, isn't it, Mother? Because you can't plan on anything. He was *only* 24 and was going to get married to that nice young girl from Rockford," Willie said. That evening Willie wrote another letter to Henry Remann. Henry had been asking for one. Willie had heard that his friend Edward McClernand's mother (Sarah Freeman (Dunlap) McClernand December 24, 1824 - May 8, 1861) had died and asked him to convey his condolences. Willie also told Henry about the tragic murder of the Lincolns' beloved friend and patriot, Col. Elmer E. Ellsworth, who had been killed by the secesch Jackson in the Marshall House in Alexandria while carrying the rebel flag he had taken down from the roof and how Ellsworth's comrade Francis Edwin Brownell (July 18, 1840 - March 15, 1894) immediately killed Jackson.

Willie said he and Tad went to church for very different reasons. Willie wanted to be a preacher when he grew up and was very conscientious especially in regard to the Sabbath. Willie prayed that day for the soul of Col. Ellsworth and that he would meet him again someday in heaven. Tad went to church to be with Willie and see what mischief he could cause. Lincoln told Tad, who had complained about having to go, "Every educated person should know something of the Bible and Bible stories." Miss Harriet *"Hattie" Almira Waller (1842 - November 22, 1861) was assigned the task of teaching Sunday School lessons at the New York Ave, Presbyterian Church. There were a lot of hard words in them but Willie buckled down and learned.

*Sources had listed her name as "Mattie", but I verified through Ancestry.com and Findagrave.com that it was actually Hattie.

Willie and Tad also liked going to the Taft's church, the Fourth

46

Street Presbyterian sometimes instead of their own. Some people in the congregation didn't like when Dr. Smith, (John Cross Smith 1810 -January 23, 1878) the pastor, prayed for Lincoln. They got up and left banging the pew doors. They were secesch. Tad piped up, "If I were secesch, I wouldn't let Dr. Smith stop me from banging pew doors." Willie retorted, "Yes, and get put in the Guard House!" Willie asked Julie who had accompanied Willie and Tad if she thought Dr. Smith would pray for them too and she said she was sure he would. Then Willie noticed that Dr. Smith did see and recognize them and Willie's face turned red with embarrassment.

Willie, Tad, Julie and the boys were playing in the Sitting Room in the Mansion when Abe and Mary asked Julie why Willie and Tad liked to go to her church. Julie answered, "I reckon our church is livelier." Mary asked Willie, "Do you think it's livelier, Willie?" Willie replied, "Oh, yes, lot's livelier! Only maybe it won't be as lively anymore. The seceshes used to leave and bang the pew doors while Dr. Smith was praying for father but now the Provost Guard comes and the lieutenant threatens to arrest them and take them to the Guard House."

On May 30th at 3 o'clock Lincoln reviewed troops of the 9th and 14th New York Regiments, the German Regiment and the Italian Garibaldi Guards, 4,000 in all. Willie ran into Julie and asked about Bud. She said all three of the boys were sick.

June 1st Mary went to New York to buy some furnishing for the Mansion. She was always buying furniture and clothes and Lincoln used to argue with her about over- spending the budget for such things but she didn't pay any attention. It was a habit she couldn't stop [she was most likely a shopaholic and possibly bipolar with her mood swings]. She was worried Willie and Tad would be too lonely while she was away and she asked Mrs. Taft if Bud and Holly could stay with them at the Mansion while she was gone and so Abe could have company at meals. That morning before Mary had sent the mes-senger to the Taft's to ask Mrs. Taft to let the boys stay over, Willie and Tad had gone exploring in the Capitol building. They listened in the gallery of the House of Representatives till Tad complained it was boring. Then some gentlemen treated the boys to lunch at the Restaurant of Congress. Then they met some of the pages who were about Bud's age and they played marbles with the boys in the hallway. Tad at least played with success for marbles were fairly bursting from his pockets.

When they got back to the Mansion it was raining real hard and they were ready to go over to the Taft's to get Bud and Holly so they searched around for an umbrella and borrowed an old dilapidated one from the cook. It didn't do much good anyway and by the time they got to L Street they were like soaked, muddy rats but they didn't care. All they could think of was the great fun they were going to have with Bud and Holly at the Mansion. As they left the Taft's lugging the satchel with Bud and Holly's things, Tad yelled back, "You bet we're gonna' have a good time!"

Julie came over to the Mansion with clean blouses for her brothers and she wondered why all the servants were grinning broadly. Willie had organized a circus that the boys were putting on in the attic. About a week previously the boys had attended a minstrel show and loved it and wanted to be minstrels too. They pinned a curtain of sheets across part of the attic. The circus was to be in three parts: I. PART consisting of six songs song by various members of the troupe. II. PART a banjo solo, two songs and two acting skits and III. PART Tad playing the "Black Statue." Willie was glad Julie came as he and Bud were to be lovely Victorian ladies and were struggling into dresses they borrowed from Mrs. Lincoln's closet. Julie pinned-up the train on Willie's with the full, long skirt with flounces of lilac silk that his mother wore on afternoon receptions and the billowy festoons on Mary's morning wrapper Bud was wearing and straightened his bonnet. Then, at the boys' request she daubed them liberally with a perfume they had also borrowed from Mary's room called "Bloom of Youth." Willie said, "Boy does it reek!" The audience consisted of servants, orderlies, soldiers, children and whoever else could muster-up the five cents admission charge. However, J. King who was the Proprieteur [French spelling popular at the time] of Admissions left them in for one cent if that's all they had. Bud, Holly, Willie Taft and other friends: Billy Sanders (William A. Sanders 1845 - June 16, 1871), *Joe Corkhead, John King (1850 - 1927), C. Donelson (Christopher Columbus F. Donelson 1851 - December 18, 1844) and John Small (John H. Small September 1855 - ?) were in the troupe. Tad, was to play the part of the "Black Statue" in III. PART. When Julie arrived Tad said he wanted to use a bottle of shoe polish but she took it away from him and made him up with burnt cork instead. Willie had printed a Programme [French spelling popular at the time] and they were soon ready to begin the show. They opened with a rousing edition of "Hail Columbia." Billy Sanders and Tad then sang "The Star-Bangles Banner." "Dixieland" followed sung by Joe Corkhead and Bud in Mary's white morning gown and stylish bonnet and then Willie in the voluminous, lilac silk gown and J. King sang "Home Sweet Home." That seemed to bring the audience to tears. Willie shed a few tears himself thinking of his home back on 8th Street in Springfield. In that same moment Willie felt a flash of sadness. It passed as soon as it came. C. Donelson and Holly ended I. PART with "Red, White And Blue." II. PART began with a banjo solo by Billy Sanders and Joe Corkhead, the "Champion of Peace" by Billy Sanders continuing with "I Am Going, And I Am Gone" by John Small and Joe Corkhead. Tad had wanted to sing "Old Abe Lincoln Came Out Of The Wilderness" but Willie talked him out of it. It didn't seemed respectful to Willie now that their father was president. The two skits "Stocks Up And Stocks Down" and "The Steam Arm" performed by Joe Corkhead, Billy Sanders and J. King ended II. PART. The III. PART concluded with "The Black Statue" by Tad which was a great success. John Hay came up to the attic mad at the boys as usual wanting to know if they had taken their father's spectacles. Tad had borrowed them for the show and reluctantly turned them over to Hay and asked Julie to get a pair from an old gentleman who was visiting and had two. She didn't. Then Abe came up to the attic and he enjoyed the show hugely. He said to the boys, "I see you're having a great time up here."

*I couldn't find any record of a "Corkhead" in Ancestry.com or Findagrave.com in the U.S. The name Corkhead does appear in Gloucestershire, England. Joe's parents may have been members of the English diplomatic corp. living temporarily in Washington. and not picked up by the census, city directory, etc.

On June 4th the 79th Scottish Highlands Regiment arrived early in the morning and although it rained some, marched down Pennsylvania Avenue playing "The Campbells Are Coming." It was a stirring spectacle and four of the boys [Bud and Holly were still staying at the Mansion] enjoyed it very much. In the afternoon the boys went over to the Taft's with the "Programe" from their minstrel-circus and asked Julie to correct it. Willie had left out the second 'm" in Programme which she inserted and the real names of the actors Willie had left out. Willie and Bud both made copies and left the original in Julie's portfolio together with a copy Tad began to make. But after drawing a picture of General [Winfield] Scott he gave up the task.

The dry weather of June brought the great dust. The only street that was paved was Pennsylvania Avenue and dust got in their clothes, noses, mouths and food more than back home in Springfield. It was impossible. As much as Willie hated the muddy streets of the other seasons, this was worse. Willie said the whole town smelled like ten thousand dead animals from the putrid canal, swamps south of the Mansion and the Potomac itself that was used as an open latrine by the thousands of troops near it. Washington's population had swelled from 30,000 in 1860 to over 100,000 by June of 1861. Lincoln told Willie people actually did throw dead animals in the canal. Flies and mosquitoes ate the Lincolns up too.

June 14th Abe, Willie and Tad went to the B&O train depot in the afternoon to meet their mother returning from New York via Philadelphia after her shopping trip. Bud and Holly returned home.

A few days later Willie went over to the Taft's to see Bud who told him of his morning visit the previous day to the Marshall House in

Alexandria where Col. Ellsworth was killed. Bud said they also visited the camps of the Michigan Regiment and the Zouaves on "Shooters Hill" about a mile back of the city. Willie wished he'd have gone along but it would have been very sad to see where his beloved friend was killed. Bud said there was still traces of blood on the stairs where the deed had been done.

June 17th was a nice summer day and not as hot and humid as it sometimes gets in Washington. Bud was sick and Tad and Holly were off playing somewhere so Willie went out and lay down in the cool, green grass on the front lawn. He looked up at the moving clouds imagining that they were shapes of animals. He went over words in his mind that described the clouds. Willie had already written some poems but didn't think they were very good. Lincoln had written some poems when he was a boy and Willie wanted to be like his father. And like his father, Willie liked to read everything he could get his hands on. Willie thought that the chief advantage of being president was being able to read all day in the library, however, he realized that his father was way too busy to do that. But Willie made up for it. Willie had never seen so many books and magazines that were in the library. Willie picked up the *Atlantic Monthly* and found a humorous description of Washington:

"The houses are low, the rents high; the hacks are black, the horses white; the squares are triangles, except that of the capitol, which is oval, If the beggars of Dublin, the cripples of Constantinople, and the lepers of Damascus should assemble in Baden-Baden during the Congress of Kings, then Baden-Baden would resemble Washington. Society in Washington dresses as it pleases and does as little work as possible. It's only trouble is lack of money. Everybody is busted. It is not an isolated complaint."

June 21st Mary Lincoln, Cousin Lizzie, Willie and Tad accompanied by General Hiram Walbridge (February 2, 1821 - December 6, 1870) were driving in the Lincoln's carriage over to Virginia to have a look at the camps when the horses stumbled and fell throwing their driver out of the box and breaking the pole. They all held on to their seats except for Tad who would have been crushed by a wheel had it not been for the quick action of General Walbridge who grabbed him as he was about to tumble out.

Willie and Tad were playing in Lafayette Square when a boy called them "mudsills." Willie and Tad weren't sure what it meant but it didn't sound nice and Tad wanted to punch the boy but Bud who was also there and Willie, restrained him. Willie told Tad it would get in the papers and embarrass their father. Willie learned later it meant *the lowest windowsill of the house, the one embedded in mud or lowest strata of society.* That boy had expressed an opinion very prevalent in Washington. The Lincolns were looked down upon because they were from the "wild West of Illinois" [hardly very far west] and called Lincoln a railsplitter. So, what's wrong with that Willie thought. Willie guessed that their clothes [baggy wool suits] were different but they were comfortable. Willie reckoned that some people were jealous because Lincoln got to be president.

Sunday, June 23rd after church and lunch, Lincoln announced that since it was a nice summer day cool and sunny, the family would go to visit Francis Preston Blair (April 12, 1791 - October 18, 1876), a friend of Lincoln's who lived seven miles north of Washington at Silver Springs in Maryland. Abe said it was a magnificent place with four or five hundred acres and the boys would have a great time exploring in the wide open spaces, free of the summer stink and dust of Washington. Mr. Blair had eight grandchildren and along with Willie and Tad played town ball [early form of baseball] for hours on the vast lawn. Lincoln joined in running with his long strides, his coattails sticking out behind and how the boys tried to hit him with the ball as he ran the bases [a player was out if he was hit by a ball thrown by the other team and there were no gloves]. Abe entered into the spirit of the play as much as any of the boys and they invariably hailed his playing with delight.

Bud and Holly's blouses got mixed up with Willies and Tad's from when they stayed over at the Mansion and theirs were left there. Willie and Tad wanted to attend a state dinner with their parents and Mary said OK as long as they wore Buds and Holly's blouses They fit Willie and Tad because although Bud and Holly were older they were about the same size. Willie thought his father looked pretty plain in his black suit but Mary was dressed up in her best finery.

Lincoln said there was bad news from Fortress Monroe [Old Point Comfort, Virginia] with considerable loss on both sides in a fierce fight.

The next day Bud came to the Mansion about 10 and he. Willie and Tad gathered their "troops," drilled, marched and had skirmishes. In the afternoon they went to the various encampments in the President's Park and on the front lawn talking to the soldiers. Holly didn't come with Bud that day as he had accompanied his Sunday School teacher to the Navy Yard and was to have tea with him.

Tad broke a large looking-glass [mirror] in the vestibule with a new ball he'd just received. He tried to say his father wouldn't care. Willie told him, "It's not father's looking-glass. It belongs to the United States government." The noise of the broken glass brought Julie, Bud and Holly from another room. Julie was horrified. She said to Tad, "I suppose you know you're in for nothing but bad luck for five years." "Because I broke that old looking-glass?" Tad tried to sound like he wasn't worried but Willie remembered and he was sure Tad remembered hearing Mrs. Keckly who had many superstitions say the same thing. I advise you to throw salt over your left shoulder and say the Lord's Prayer backwards," Julie said coldly. Tad darted into the family room and came back with a whole handful of salt. The he tossed it over his left shoulder on to the velvet carpet. "Now for the Lord's Prayer," Bud said. "That means you start with amen," Holly added. "Tad doesn't even know it forward. He's still at 'Our Father who art…'" Willie said. "I do so know it," Tad cried. "I reckon I've been to church as often as you… amen…ever…and…" a long pause, "Forever," Bud prompted. "Now you've spoiled it!" Julie yelled at her brother. "Tad, start over again," Julie continued. "Aw, let it slide. What can happen anyway. My father's president." Holly was impressed with Tad's *courage* and said, "You're going to dare five years of bad luck, Tad?" Tad nodded and said, "Let's go play outside," changing the subject.

The Lincolns had lots of pets at the Mansion that people gave them. Jip, Abe's little dog, had pups and Willie ran to tell his father where he had been talking to some man (Moncure Daniel Conway May 17, 1832 - November 15, 1907) representing a delegation. Then five minutes later Tad came running to tell that the cat had kittens. Abe laughed and was as happy as the boys and said he would come see them as soon as he was done talking.

Two Rhode Island regiments with their two batteries, 12:12 pounders, were reviewed by Lincoln the next evening.

Willie, Tad and the Taft boys decided to see if they could climb up the curtains in the East Room to try to get up and sit on the valance covers up there which they did. Just then Abe came in with a group of gentlemen, his Cabinet, for a meeting. The boys didn't dare let out a peep and had to stay up there as quiet as mice through the whole meeting after which they slid down and nobody was the wiser but it was a close call. Willie thought Abe would have thought it "smart" [not the Cabinet, especially Stanton] as he did back in March when they disrupted a Cabinet meeting shooting off caps from their cannon.

Tad was fascinated by money and hoarded it and was not particular how he made it. He bet Secretary Seward (William Henry Seward May 16, 1801 - October 10, 1872) a quarter that he could not guess what new animal he and Willie had just received. Secretary Seward guessed a rabbit. Tad shook his head, pocketed his money and left in a hurry. Willie gravely told the Secretary that indeed it had been a rabbit.

Senator Dawes (Henry Laurens Dawes October 30, 1816 - February 5, 1903) gave Willie and Tad dozens of marbles all of them ending up in Tad's pockets before the day was out.

June 29th Bud and the whole Taft family came to the Mansion to watch the raising of the Stars and Stripes at a tent on the lawn. It got caught going up and was torn among the stars which was taken by superstitious people in the crowd as a bad omen. Abe said to not pay any attention to those people as it was just the wind.

Lincoln would like nothing better than to play with his sons but sometimes Willie would say, "Father doesn't have time to play with us now." Willie understood he was very busy being president and tending to war matters but Willie really missed the times in Springfield. That day, June 30th, was different. He had time. Willie sat on one knee, Bud on the other. Holly was on the arm of the chair. Tad perched on the back of the chair. Abe then recounted exciting tales of hunters, settlers and Indians; stories he had heard as a boy in old Kentucky. When Julie came, Abe's long arm drew her into the circle. Lincoln always wanted a daughter but had four boys instead and he looked at Julie as he did Josie Remann back home in Springfield as the daughter he never had and loved her. Willie had a crush on Julie but Willie was only ten and Julie was sixteen and swooned over the older boys like she had over Col. Ellsworth [all the girls had] and other young officers. After the stories Abe would wrestle with the boys. He got down on the floor and the boys tried to hold him down. Willie and Bud holding his arms, Tad and Holly sprawled over his legs. Julie was shocked by this, left and closed the door. She could be pretty prim and proper at times. Abe, Willie and Tad would find ways to tease her about that.

The boys had a great time against the backdrop of the war, however, Willie and Tad realized more of the sadness and tragedy of it all, but they didn't want to dwell on that part, on all that killing, especially after the death of their beloved Ellsworth.

July 3rd a brilliant comet [later called the War Comet or the Great Comet of 1861 discovered by Australian astronomer John Tebbutt May 25, 1834 - November 29, 1916] appeared in the sky that evening and was quite a spectacle. Willie had seen meteors before but nothing as bright as that.

Lincoln received a request from Horatio Nelson Taft, Sr., Bud's father, asking if Abe would favor Bud's application to become a page in the House of Representatives. Abe said he would and asked Willie what he thought about it. Willie told him that Bud was fourteen and was old enough and very capable although he added that he would miss playing with him as he would be busy with page work.

July 4th there was a huge parade with many regiments and bands playing "On To Richmond" the secesch capital. There were German regiments of Frederick's [The Great] tradition singing *"Ach du liber Augustin"* and Luther' grand hymn *"Ein Feste Burg."* There was the 69th New York Irish born who bore the green flag of Erin with Stars and Stripes and the 79th New York, the Highlanders with their kilts and bagpipes. Then came the French regiment, the 55th, singing *"Aux Armes Citoyens."* Other regiments chanted "John Brown's Body" all with flags flying and guns wreathed in flowers. At lease 21,000 troops passed in review. That evening there was a wonderful show of crackers [firecrackers]. Willie and Tad put off their own on the lawn.

On Wednesday and Saturday evenings the Marine Band gave concerts on the Mansion lawn in a large tent made with 508 yards of "duck" [a heavy, plain-weave cotton fabric for tents].

Robert Lincoln got the mumps at Harvard. Willie wrote to him after Mary Lincoln went to see Bob. Abe said Willie is getting quite good at writing and better than a lot of adults.

Lincoln took Willie, Tad, Bud and Holly along with him to General McClellan's (George Brinton McClellan December 3, 1826 - October 29, 1885) Headquarters to see his baby daughter. Both the General and Mrs. McClellan (Mary Ellen [Marcy] McClellan May 6, 1835 - February 13, 1915) were very kind to the boys. The boys played with the baby whom Bud was very fond of.

Willie noticed a huge balloon over the city and asked his father what it was. Lincoln explained that a man named Thaddeus Sobieski Coulincourt Lowe (August 20, 1832 - January 16, 1913) had made and it was going to be used to locate enemy positions. Willie wished he could ride in it.

July 12th Willie and the boys went to the Patent Office where Bud's father worked to see the models of locomotives and steamboats there.

Tad received a gift of a doll dressed like a Zouave. He named it Private Jack. "He" was a deserter and the boys had a court martial for him and executed him [several times] in Major John Watt's (John Watt (1824 - 1892) rose garden. Watt was not happy and still mad at Tad for the strawberry incident among others. Watt suggested they pardon Jack and the boys appealed to Lincoln who wrote an official paper, "The Doll Jack is pardoned by order of President A. Lincoln." However, in less than a week the boys found Jack guilty of spying but this time hung him from a tree in Bud's family garden. After each execution they held a "dead march" with an old broken fiddle, banged-up horn, a paper over a comb and Tad's drum.

Abe and Mary took Willie and Tad along with them to visit the camps and took fruit, candy and cakes to the soldiers.

Willie and the boys made a "survey" of the Mansion grounds under the guidance of a good-natured engineer who was working there.

Bud came to the Mansion in the morning and told Willie that his father said that he (Bud) had walked in his sleep and that he somehow got out of a third story window on to the roof of the back wing two stories high. Bus said his father got him back in without incident. Bud said he didn't remember a thing about it. Willie told Bud he was worried about him falling and that maybe he'd better tie a bell to his ankle so it wakes him up if he starts to get out of his bed in his sleep.

Sunday, July 21st Willie and Tad went to the Taft's to wait for the Taft children to come home from Sunday School. When they came Willie told them excitedly, "Father says there's a battle in Virginia. That noise is big cannons going off that sounds like slamming doors." Willie was flushed and wild with excitement. It was the Battle of Manassas Junction [Bull Run] in full progress. When Willie and Tad got back to the Mansion they made their way to the roof by the steep stairs. Mary Lincoln and their cousin Lizzie Grimsley joined them. Puffs of smoke and flashes of fire shown through the pale, hazy morning sky. Mary was looking through a telescope. Tad yelled that he wanted to look and his mother pushed his hand away. Tad howled. "Serves you right.," Willie said. "Say please," Tad told Willie to shut up and kicked him in the shin. Willie grabbed him. Lizzie told the boys to stop grabbing each of them by one arm and said, "Imagine, scuffling up here with no railing or anything." Of course she didn't know the boys played up there all the time. Lincoln came up to the roof. "Do you know any of the soldiers, you know, like poor Ellsworth?" Willie asked. Abe and Mary looked at each other. "I can't say that we do," Abe answered after what seemed a long time. "Of course there's General McDowell, (Irwin McDowell October 15, 1818 - May 4, 1885), we all know him." "I mean boys," Willie said. Willie understood the difference with the older men stout with gray beards and gray in their hair and the others with hair all one color [like Ellsworth's jet black hair] who still liked to play games with ten-year-olds, wrestle and laugh. "No." Mary seemed very serious. "We don't know any of them." Willie thought that his mother believed if the boys didn't know any of them they wouldn't be sad and grieve for them when they are killed in battle. "What about the southern boys? The ones from Kentucky?" Willie asked not giving up. His mother looked at him kind of sadly and putting her around him said, "Come on to breakfast." Willie noticed that he was almost as tall as his mother. He had grown a few inches in the past year. He thought he would be tall like his father. They had breakfast and everyone was quiet except Tad who didn't understand the gravity of what was happening to all those boys a few miles away in Virginia. The whole Lincoln family went to church at the New York Avenue Presbyterian and Willie prayed hard for the Union troops and all the widows and children who would be grieving that night and always.

The next day, July 22nd was a sad, rainy morning. General Scott came to the Mansion and urged Mary to take the boys north but since Lincoln wouldn't go too, they all stayed. Willie told his mother not to worry as he, Tad and the Taft boys would defend the Mansion along with the New York and Pennsylvania troops bivouacked on the grounds. Lincoln smiled and said, "I know you will son." Lincoln sent a telegram ordering General George McClellan to take command of the

Army of the Potomac. Lincoln had become friends when McClellan had been president of the Illinois Central Railroad before the war and Abe was solicitor for the railroad.

Willie and the boys wanted to help with guarding the Mansion so they made their own fort on the roof. They used a small log for a cannon, a couple of old rifles that couldn't fire and peered through an old spyglass for signs of "enemy cruisers" coming up the Potomac to bombard the city. Willie had heard there was a threat of an enemy Naval invasion. Willie organized a battalion that he called "Mr. Lincoln's Zouaves" in honor of the late beloved Ellsworth. Willie was colonel; Bud, major; Holly, captain; and Tad who naturally liked the noisy part, drum major. General McClellan had given the "officers" some old-fashioned swords with stern warnings to be careful with them.

Willie loved to write and kept a *box hidden in the library with little sermons and speeches he had written, railroad timetables he had created, attempts at poetry, newspaper clippings of battles and other important events such as the inauguration of Richard Yates (January 8, 1815 - November 27, 1873) as governor of Illinois on January 14, 1861 right before the Lincolns left for Washington. Governor Yates was a good friend of the Lincolns.

The *box mentioned above was discovered by Lincoln after Willie's death and shown to Abe's friend Orville Hickman Browning (February 10, 1806 - August 10, 1881) one Sunday in June 1862. The box disappeared after Lincoln's assassination [probably thrown out in April 1865 by Mary Lincoln who could not bear, sadly, to keep anything of Willie's as they were too painful a reminder]. Had the box of Willie's "memoranda" as Lincoln called it, survived, it would have been an invaluable window into the heart and mind of the gifted, precocious, special son of Abraham Lincoln,

August 1st Willie got to meet Prince Napoleon Joseph Charles Bonaparte (September 9, 1822 - March 14, 1891), Lucien Bonaparte's son and nephew of Napoleon III and Eugenie. Willie was on the sidewalk in front of the Mansion when Secretary Seward and the Prince drove up in a barouche. To Willie's surprise and delight they both took off their hats and saluted him. Willie was a little embarrassed as he was not used to that sort of greeting but drew himself up to his full height, took off his cap and bowed down to the very ground. The Prince was very impressive in his full dress with many decorations and a broad crimson sash.

Willie tried to be like his father who was very popular with adults and children alike Willie would approach people, shake hands and try to say something nice. Abe was good to people and that made him happy and Willie happy. The frequent Mansion visitor Nathaniel Parker Willis (January 20, 1806 - January 20, 1867), a publisher and poet and frequent editor and founder of several periodicals, including the *Home Journal*, now published as *Town and Country* and who worked with several well known literary figures including Edgar Allan Poe and Henry Wadsworth Longfellow, described Willie thusly, "His well-balanced nature was developing beautifully in spite of the war setting he was growing up in. With everything going around him and the splendor of his new home, he was bravely and beautifully himself. Willie had a fearless and kindly frankness willing that everything be as different as it pleased but resting unmoved in his own conscious single-heartedness." Willie thought at first he was describing his father and was not exactly sure what Willis meant and *why* all the praise when he was just being himself.

Willie and Tad were up early and went over to the Taft's and played with the boys under the shade of the big tree in their back yard. They reconstructed battles which of course the Union always won. It was already in the 90s by ten o'clock and the boys were glad for the delicious lemonade Mrs. Taft brought out to them. Later they went to Gautier's (James M. Gautier January 27, 1836 - January 22, 1911) for ice cream.

Willie and Tad went to see the Zouave uniforms Mrs. Taft had made for Bud, Holly and little Willie. Willie and Tad had their regular blue soldier uniforms on and they all marched around in formation drilling. On the way back to the Mansion Tad fussed that they, Tad and

Willie, had to have "Zouaves" too. Willie told him, "Be thankful for what you have, Tad Lincoln."

August 9th wasn't as hot. It had been in the 90s all week and Willie missed the swimming holes in the Sangamon River and Spring Creek back in Springfield. They can't swim in Washington as the Potomac and Tiber are cesspools. At the Taft's the boys constructed a bivouac tent camp-style, played army and stood guard duty in case the secesch invaded the neighborhood.

General Scott and General McClellan didn't get along and Lincoln tried his best to make them work together for the sake of the Union. Prince Napoleon left to return to France August 10th.

Julie, Bud and Holly came to the Mansion and Julie told a story about a fat girl who wouldn't tell her weight and Abe overheard and re-told it. She (the fat girl) sat at the very end of the bus and everyone got out except the fat girl. The driver hurriedly drove the bus to a hay scale and weighed it with her in it. Then the girl got out and he weighed it again. Willie said to Julie, "I heard Father tell your story about the fat girl today." Julie was curious as to how it came about. Willie replied, "Why, father was talking to some men about the war and one of them said he wished he knew how big an army the rebels had in Virginia. Father said why didn't they find out. The man said they tried to. Then father told them your story about weighing the fat girl."

Willie and Tad played a lot at the Taft's because they had more freedom there. At the Mansion with all the servants, messengers, guards, Pinkerton men, Lincoln's secretaries Hay and Nicolay and Watt the gardener often interfered. At the Taft's they made a rifle pit in the garden and turned a vacant room in the attic in to "Old Capitol Prison," where much to the poor creatures' distress, they shut up Julie's cat and a neighbor's dog. They made so much noise the boys "pardoned" them when Mrs. Taft came to see what the ruckus was about.

Willie and Tad went to the Taft's and played war. The took praying mantises from the grapevine in the backyard and rubbed their noses together so they would fight. One would be a rebel and one a Zouave.

Sunday August 16th after church Willie and Tad went with Mr. Taft, Bud and Holly to visit the camps. Mr. Taft always carried with him a basket of apples, oranges or the soldiers favorite large, white onions. It was a special treat from their rations of salt horse (beef), hardtack and coffee. Willie enjoyed meeting all the (soldier) boys except for the fact that they all made a big deal about their being sons of the president. Willie thought, we're just boys, too.

Tad bugged everyone about wanting what he called a "real revolver." Julie let him hold hers and he pointed it at Bud. Julie and Willie were both very angry. Julie grabbed it and incensed, yelled at Tad, "You're not fit to have a revolver, Tad Lincoln!" On the way home from the Taft's later that day Willie said to Tad, " What if you'd pulled the trigger and killed Bud, how would you feel?" Tad started crying and said, "I give my "after-David" (he meant affidavit) I'll never point it at anyone again!"

August 19th Mary, Willie, Tad and Bob who came down from Harvard, Cousin Lizzie, Mary's friend and their former neighbor from Springfield, Mrs. John Shearer (Hannah [Miner Rathbun] Shearer August 22, 1828 - October 20, 1879) and her two boys Edward "Eddie" Rathbun, Jr. (1848 - 1862), James Miner Rathbun (1853 - August 5, 1898) and John Hay traveled to the seashore at Long Branch, [the Atlantic City of its time catering to the rich and famous] New Jersey. Willie was overjoyed at seeing Eddie who had next to Henry Remann, been his best friend in Springfield before Eddie and his family had moved in 1859 to Wellsboro, Pennsylvania due to Eddie's stepfather's (Dr. John Henry Shearer (January 16, 1827 - December 19, 1898) tubercular condition. Willie and Tad had never seen the ocean before except in magazines and briefly from a distance in New York. It was gloomy and raining their first day there and they were cooped up in their hotel rooms. Willie, Tad, Eddie and James were bored and wanted to explore the beach. The hotel was called the Mansion House which Willie thought was an appropriate name as they were the president's family and came from the Executive Mansion. That evening they had lots of visitors; mostly young ladies who surrounded Bob. Mrs. Shearer, who was pregnant, became quite sick and was confined to her bed.

The next morning the weather was somewhat improved. Willie and Tad begged their mother to let them go out and when there was a brief lull in the storm they were able to visit the cricket grounds and watch the match between Long Branch and St. George. They were only there a few minutes when the rain started again and Mary said they had to go back to the hotel. After dinner the weather improved again and Mary decided they should take a drive with the daughter of Judge (?) White. Willie found out that evening that Long Branch lost the cricket match to St. George. All said it had been a fierce contest.

The next day, August 22nd, they were finally able to go to the beach although the weather was still very changeable, half the time sunshiny and half the time windy, stormy and dust-raising. Willie, Tad, Eddie and James quickly got into their bathing suits but the ladies had to get dressed covered from head to foot in long, wool bathing dresses and caps and they had to get down to the beach inside bathhouses on wheels. They were called "bathing machines" and then the whole bathhouse with them inside was lowered down the beach on tracks with a windlass [device for raising or hauling objects]. When the whole bathhouse was lowered into the water, the ladies would get out and slosh around some. That didn't seem like much fun to Willie and the boys. They frolicked in the ocean and Willie almost stepped on a jellyfish that people said was poison. Willie had to watch Tad as was his reckless nature, kept wanting to wade too far out. Willie told him the undertow would get him and take him to France under the water. Then Tad got knocked down by a big wave and settled closer to shore as Mary was yelling at him also. The boys made sandcastles and a model of the Executive Mansion and some boy ran by and stepped on it. Tad wanted to chase him and punch him but Willie caught him in time. Willie collected seashells and one called a conch that if you held it up to your ear you could hear the ocean. That afternoon, escorted by former New Jersey Governor William Augustus. Newell (September 5, 1817

- August 8, 1901) Mary and the boys attended a demonstration of lifesaving equipment. There were 28 lifesaving stations along the Jersey shore from Sandy Hook to Egg Harbor. At each of these stations were lifeboats, life cars, mortars, rockets and all the necessary paraphernalia used at the time in 1861. Each station had a guard of ten men ready at a moment's notice. They also got to witness a demonstration of the method used by the Coast Guard to rescue people from vessels in distress. A lifeboat was launched and skillfully steered beyond the line of breakers where it lay anchor. Then the mortar was charged and fired. The ball with the line attached fell near the lifeboat and was seized by the crew who hauled in the hawser [a heavy rope for mooring or towing] connected with the surf car and then the men on the shore ran the metallic life box backwards and forwards through the surf.

That evening Willie wrote to Henry and Edward McClernand, another friend back in Springfield, and asked how the boys back home were getting along and told of the fun he and Tad had and how nice it was to see all the people bathing at the beach that was so nearby their hotel. Tad came down with a cold and stayed in the rest of the evening.

Also that evening Bob went to the "Grand Hop" that Gov. Newell held in honor of Mrs. Lincoln. [Curiously, "hop" was the same name given to teenage dances 100 years later in 1961 popularized by the song "At the Hop" by Danny and the Juniors]. Bob said he had a great time waltzing and polkaing with the young ladies. The newspapers called Bob "The Prince of Rails" either because he was the son of the "rail splitter" or because he rode the trains a lot.

Mary told Willie that they may leave tomorrow (Friday) to go to Newport, Rhode Island where Mr. Nicolay was vacationing. Mrs. Shearer has named her soon to be born baby if a boy William Lincoln Shearer (October 28, 1861 - March 31, 1932), after Willie. Willie was quite proud that someone would want to. The *Wellsboro Gazette*, March 31, 1932, reported that Col. Henry W. Shoemaker (August 26, 1864 - 1935), prominent Pennsylvania author and present ambassador to Bulgaria writes, "Writers of obituary notices of the late William

Lincoln Shearer, fames journalist and complier of *North Tier Notes*, which were one of the outstanding features of the old *Philadelphia American*, omitted that he was also the author of many brilliant editorials in that paper which attracted widespread attention all over Pennsylvania. Will Shearer loved writing for the joy it brought him and the possible good it might do. He was loyal to his friends and his character was composed without a single trait of meanness or pettiness. Will Shearer was an exceptional soul, and he left the world better for having lived in it." It is interesting to note that Willie Lincoln's namesake may have mirrored what Willie himself might become and accomplished as Willie was already a good writer at the age of 11, empathic and caring for others.

August 23rd it was decided that instead of going to Newport, they would take the New York Central Railroad across New York state stopping first at Auburn and then a courtesy call at the Seward home in Saratoga and on to Niagara Falls but would not leave till the next day due to the fact that both Mrs. Shearer and Tad are sick.

August 24th the party left Long Branch. Tad and Mrs. Shearer were better.

August 27th they traveled from Albany to Auburn accompanied by Secretary Seward.. Willie loved trains and was making his own accurate timetable to see if it matched the railroad's. They arrived in Saratoga at 10:03 a.m. just two minutes off schedule Willie noted. They stayed overnight visiting the Seward family.

August 28th they arrived in Niagara Falls and stayed at the International Hotel. Cousin Lizzie, Bob and Mrs. Shearer and the boys accompanied them this far.

August 29th.. The Falls seemed to make Tad, Mrs. Shearer and everyone feel better, happier and in a good mood. The tremendous noise and power of the water rushing over the falls and the mist and rainbow-effect was awe-inspiring, beautiful and peaceful and soothing at the same time.

August 30th they visited the Niagara Falls Museum on the Canadian side as the Lincolns had done in July 1857. It still had the Egyptian mummy Willie remembered from the earlier visit and more oddities and curiosities of nature like the Barnum Museum in New York they had visited in February on their way to Washington. [The same museum now houses barrels and other artifacts related to the history of daredevils going over the falls and tight roping across it. The current owner still has the guest book that was signed "A. Lincoln and Family" with "P. T. Barnum" (Phineas Taylor Barnum July 5, 1810 - April 17, 189 on the same page in July 1857. [See photocopy of page].

On September 2nd Bob left to return to Harvard. Cousin Lizzie, who said she missed her family, left for Kentucky and Mrs. Shearer, Eddie and James left to return home to Wellsboro, Pennsylvania. Sadly, Edward "Eddie" Rathbun, Jr. would die in Wellsboro possibly of tuberculosis contracted from his step-father. This occurred in 1862 according to the cemetery record of the Wood Lawn Cemetery, Wellsville, Allegany County, New York, where he is buried next to his father Edward Rathbun, Sr. (September 17, 1823 - May 15, 1854), who was Hannah Shearer's first husband.. His father has a large vertical stone and Eddie, his brother James who died August 5, 1898, James' wife and their daughter have a flat marker. Mary Lincoln in a letter to Mrs. Shearer in November 1864 states, "Doubtless ere this, our angel boys are reunited for they loved each other (Willie & Eddie) so much on earth."

That same day (September 2nd) Mary, Willie and Tad left for Washington.

September 4th they arrived back in Washington at the B & O Station. Willie noticed Mr. Lowe's balloon up over the Potomac on the lookout for rebels and Abe said the newspapers were reporting that Jefferson Davis was dead but Lincoln didn't believe it nor did Willie.

Secretary Seward brought the Lincolns a box of new kittens. Lincoln loved cats and missed the four kittens they had earlier that year, A few had died and the rest had been given away. These kittens loved Abe and used to sleep all over him as he slept.

On September 10th Willie and Tad went over to the Taft's and Bud told them that a neighbor of his, Mrs. Greenhow (Rose O'Neal Greenhow 1814 - September 30, 1864) was arrested as a dangerous spy [August 23rd]. She had a little daughter (Rose [Greenhow] Duvall April 2, 1853 - September 11, 1910) eight years old that the boys felt sorry for as she didn't really understand what happened to her mother. After much pleading by Tad, the boys were allowed to go to the Greenhow place to see what was going on as long as Julie accompanied them. Mrs. Greenhow and her daughter lived at 398 16th Street West where the boys found a crowd of curiosity seekers and a detachment of Sturgis (Solomon Sturgis April 21, 1796 - October 14, 1864) Rifles, General McClellan's bodyguards, surrounding the house. Mrs. Greenhow had been removed to Old Capitol Prison and later to Richmond.

Lincoln hired Mr. Alexander Williamson (1814 - June 2, 1903), a Scotsman, to be Willie, Tad, Bud, Holly and little Willie's tutor as schools were closed in Washington because of the war. Mr. Williamson was born in Edinburgh and lived in London till he emigrated to the United States in 1855 eventually settling in Washington. He was teaching school in Washington when he came to Mary Lincoln's attention through an acquaintance Major Thomas Ludwell Alexander (October 26, 1807 - May 11, 1881) in March 1861 and she sent for Williamson to come to the Mansion. Final arrangements were made in August and Williamson began tutoring the boys about September 11th. Willie, Bud and Holly began their studies with *McGuffey's Fifth Eclectic Reader [1860]* (William Holmes McGuffey September 23, 1800 - 1873), *Wilson's Fifth Reader [1861]* and Mr. William Hughes' (1818 - March 21, 1876) *Atlas of Classical Geography [1861]*. Tad and little Willie began with *McGuffey's First Eclectic Reader.* Their classroom was set up in the State Dining Room where the boys sat around the dining table. They were give pencil, paper, stylus, slates and chalk and a blackboard was brought in. Mr. Williamson had his own desk.

September 18th Bud came to the Mansion and said his father was worried about the rebels invading Washington and was thinking of sending the family to Sag Harbor, New York [on Long Island] to live with their grandmother till the war was over. Willie told Bud he would really miss him and Tad would miss Holly too and he hoped they wouldn't leave. Willie told Bud he would talk to Abe to see what could be done.. Willie told Bud to tell his father that the president would NOT let the rebels invade Washington.

More troops were arriving every day, five to six regiments by the trains. People said an attack on Washington is imminent but Willie does not believe this as large numbers of troops have gone over the river to protect Washington.

Willie and Tad went to church at the Fourth Street Presbyterian with Mr. Taft and the boys. Willie asked him to reconsider moving as his father would protect them but he just shook his head.

September 25th Julie, Bud, Holly and little Willie came to the Mansion and along with Willie and Tad went up to the roof with Lincoln's spyglass and could see the rebel flag on Munson's Hill. Mary Lincoln was very nice to Julie and the boys and sent two beautiful bouquets of camellias home with Julie.

The next day Mrs. Taft went to the Mansion to pay her respects before the family left for Sag Harbor. Mary Lincoln assured her if there was anything she could do to keep the family in Washington she would do it as she was anxious to have the Taft boys continue to come to the Mansion as companions and playmates for Willie and Tad.

September 29th Bud and Holly came to the Mansion after church and told the Lincolns they would not have to leave the city after all and were moving to 346 9th Street West next to *Commodore Albert N. Smith. Willie was greatly relieved as he had been very sad at the possibility of losing his best friend in Washington, Bud.

*A Captain Albert N. Smith (November 20, 1822 - September 8, 1866), US Navy, is listed in the 1866 Washington City Directory as living at 348 9th St. West.

The next day Willie received another letter from his friend Henry Remann back in Springfield. Willie wrote back telling him about how his new companions were raising a battalion. Willie explained that in June he had joined another boy trying to get up a regiment. That failed so then he tried to muster a company. That broke up. Then some boy told Willie he already had a battalion and Willie's company joined believing the boy was telling the truth which turned out to not be the case. Willie wrote he was very disappointed so he and his companions went to work raising a battalion of their own which is in a high state of efficiency and discipline.

October 1st the Taft's moved to 346 9th Street West from L Street which is a little longer walk for Willie and Tad from the Mansion.

Sadly, Willie couldn't get the boys in his battalion to stay focused and they all eventually deserted leaving just four; Willie, Tad, Bud and Holly.

Mr. Lowe's balloon was high over Virginia in the evening spying on the rebs and taking pictures, Willie thought.

Willie, Tad and the Taft boys went to the Taft's in the morning after tutoring. Willie liked Mrs. Taft a lot and Tad was singing "Old Abe Lincoln, a rail-splitter was he and that's the way he'll split the Confederacee'eee-ee-e." Willie didn't think it was quite right when Tad wanted to include it in their circus and he didn't think it was quite right now, so Willie said, "Ought Tad to sing that song, Mrs. Taft? Isn't it real disrespectful to father?" Mrs. Taft said she thought it rather bad taste for the president's son to be singing that. Tad replied that his father really *did* split rails. Tad then said, "Well, I'll sing about "John Brown's Body" instead. Later when Willie thought about it, Tad *was* right and Abe would have laughed. Willie was always conscious about how his and Tad's behavior would reflect on their father. Willie didn't want anything to hurt Abe as he comes under enough criticism as it is.

October 8th Lincoln, Willie, Tad, Bud and Holly went to the Great Review that morning. Julie was there with Captain Mew (William Mew 1835 - September 19, 1902). There were 108 pieces of artillery, and 6,400 cavalry that went by in a long procession up Pennsylvania Avenue.

Willie went to the Taft's by himself as Tad was sick. Willie asked Bud why he called his father "Mr. President" but he didn't call his mother "Mrs. President." Bud replied, "Oh, it's not proper to call presidents by their names. But your mother is just Mrs. Lincoln . Only the servants call her madam."

Mr. Williamson is an excellent teacher and Willie liked him very much. Willie and Bud are doing well in their studies, Holly and little Willie alright but Tad is having difficulties. He can't stay focused very long and seems disinterested.

Tutor Williamson stated after Willie's death, "William Wallace was by far the brighter of the two [Lincoln] boys. Had he lived he would have been a great man. He was the exact counterpart of his father, but had his mother's face. His memory was so wonderfully retentive that he had only to con over once or twice a page of his speller and definer that the impression became so fixed that he went through without hesitation or blundering and his other studies in proportion. [Such was] his aptitude in mastering the studies he was pursuing."

Willie and Tad went to the Taft's in the afternoon of October 14th and Willie had a special present for Julie. He had a crush on her even though she was 16 and he was only 10. Willie knew she had looked longingly at Col. Ellsworth and now at Captain Mew and other boys but he "loved" her anyway. Willie gave her a photograph of himself and a little watch charm and said to her, "I will give you my little gold dog, Julie, because I love you and you must keep it always." Julie looked surprised for a minute, kissed Willie on the cheek and said, "I'll treasure it always, Willie, you are the most lovable boy I have ever known; bright, sweet-tempered, gentle-mannered, and always thinking of others above yourself." Willie blushed red and was very happy.

Willie and Tad never did return Bud and Holly's blouses after they stayed over at the Mansion and Willie and Tad wore them again at another state dinner. Willie said to his mother, "I've got on Bud's again." She replied, "Never mind, it fits you better than it did Bud, and yours fits him better."

Bud came to the Mansion in the morning with a note from his father for Major Watt. Bud brought his top along and Willie got his from his room and they had a fine time spinning them. Then they got some wood from out back of the Mansion and Willie tried whittling a horse but it wasn't very good. Bud had a talent for whittling and produced a fine horse and a dog. Bud also drew very well and had other artistic skills. Mary Lincoln sent Bud home with a fine bouquet from the Secretary of Interior C.B. Smith (Caleb B. Smith April 16, 1808 - January 7, 1864).

Sunday, October 20 Willie and Tad went to church with Julie and the Taft boys. Autumn had come to Washington and all the leaves had turned gold, red, and every shade in-between. In the afternoon, the Lincoln's family friend Colonel Edward Dickinson Baker (February 24, 1811 - October 21, 1861) [Willie's brother Edward "Eddy" Lincoln who died February 1, 1850 at almost four years of age of tuberculosis was named after Col. Baker] was visiting. Abe was sitting on the lawn with his back against a tree and Col. Baker stretched out next to him talking Nearby, Willie was playing in a pile of leaves. After a while Abe and Col. Baker got up and stretched. Willie had known Col. Baker since he was a toddler and he was like a favorite uncle to Willie. Edward Dickinson Baker was born in London, England and emigrated to the United States with his parents in 1815 settling in Philadelphia. He moved to Illinois in 1825, studied law, was admitted to the bar in 1830 and commenced practice in Springfield where he met and became good friends with Lincoln and his family. He was serving as Colonel of the Seventy-First Regiment, Pennsylvania Volunteers in 1861. Col. Baker smiled at Willie, lifted him up in his arms and tenderly kissed him. Then, without another word mounted his horse that had been tied nearby and rode away. Lincoln knew he was going into battle and followed him with shadowed eyes until he disappeared down Pennsylvania Avenue.

October 21st Colonel Baker was killed at the Battle of Ball's Bluff near Leesburg, Virginia. The rebels who greatly outnumbered the

Union troops and held the high ground on a bluff overlooking the Potomac on the Maryland side mowed down the almost suicidal Union soldiers in the river and trying to scale the bluff. Col. Baker somehow made it to the top fighting valiantly before being shot. A stone marker and American flag mark the spot where he fell. Willie and the whole Lincoln family were overcome with grief after this second loss of a close family friend that year. Willie would later write a poem in tribute to Col. Baker that was published in the Washington newspaper the *National Republican*.

The funeral of Col. Baker was held on October 24th. There was a great display of troops and a long procession reaching a mile or more befitting a great hero. The procession began at 12 noon at the house of James W. Webb (James Watson Webb February 8, 1802 - June 7, 1884, Ambassador to Brazil) at 12th and H Streets where Col. Baker's body had been taken. Lincoln had wanted the body taken to the East Room but the Mansion was now in the hands of the upholsterers so that course was not practicable. The procession went up 13th Street to Pennsylvania Avenue to the Congressional Burying Ground. The Lincolns followed the hearse with members of the Cabinet. The 36th Pennsylvania Volunteers, the 71st Pennsylvania Volunteers Col. Baker 's Regiment and the 4th Rhode Island Volunteers along with generals and staff of the Army of the Potomac provided the escort. The coffin containing the body was covered with black cloth, silver mounted and draped by the Stars and Stripes and loaded with beautiful wreathes of white camellias and evergreens entwined. Rev. Byron Sunderland (November 22, 1819 - June 30, 1901) of the First Presbyterian Church gave the sermon which was in the highest degree affecting and impressive and then with weeping and tremulous voice recited the life and death of the gallant deceased. Willie could not help crying and Bud who watching the proceedings with his family, put his arm around Willie.

The evening of the 26th to take their minds briefly off the tragedy of Col. Baker's death, the Lincoln family went to the Odd Fellows Hall on 7th Street above D street to see Miss Susan Denin (March 22, 1835 - December 4, 1875) in the comedy "Still Waters Run Deep" and also "Post of Honor." The show concluded with the Campbell Minstrels performing new songs, the last being "Sons of Malta."

On October 30 Willie sent the poem he wrote as a tribute to the memory of Col. Baker to the newspaper the *New Republic,*

LINES

On the Death of Colonel Edward Baker

There was no patriot like Baker,
So noble and so true;
He fell as a soldier on the field,
His face to the sky of blue.

His voice is silent in the hall,
Which oft his presence grac'd,
No more he'll hear the loud acclaim,
Which rang from place to place.

No squeamish notions filled his breast,
The *Union* was his theme,
"*No surrender and no compromise,*"
His day's thought and night's dream.

His country has *her* part to play,
To'rds those he left behind,
His widow and his children all,
She must always keep in mind.

November 1st General Winfield Scott resigned the Command of the Armies of the Union. He was old and infirm. Lincoln appointed

General George McClellan to succeed him.

November 4th Willie was awakened early in the morning by the sounds of the fire wagons' bells clanging. He found out there was a fire at the E Street Infirmary between 4th and 5th Streets. Thankfully, all escaped except one aged lady. The fire brought back memories to Willie of Col. Ellsworth's courageous, acrobatic fire-Zouaves who saved Willard's Hotel the previous May. Willie, Tad, Bud and Holly went to see the burnt building. That same day Willie was happy to see that his poem about the death of Col. Baker had been published in the *New Republic* newspaper. Above Willie's note to the editor and poem was printed the following:

"Little Willie Lincoln, son of President Lincoln, has sent us the following verses which are quite credible as a first effort for one so young [age 10]. We insert them with pleasure and hope that Willie's desire as expressed in the last verse will meet with a ready response by the whole country. It should not be forgotten that the rebels gave Mrs. Jackson [James W. murderer of Ellsworth] *one hundred thousand dollars.* Charleston alone giving twenty thousand."

Willie hadn't told his father about the poem and sending it to the newspaper because he wanted to surprise him if they printed it. Willie ran up to his father's office with the paper, "Father, there's something in the paper I want you to read!" Willie was beaming. Lincoln cleared his throat and read the poem. Abe's eyes teared-up. "I will keep and value this poem, son. These are true and feeling lines. Colonel Baker would have been proud of them. I am proud of them." Lincoln showed the poem to Secretary John Hay. "Would you suspect it!" Hay exclaimed. "That's good, sir. He's a quiet one, that boy. You never know what's going on in his head," Hay continued. Lincoln said, "Willie has *RARE LIGHTS, RARE LIGHTS!*"

They all went to see King's National Circus at R Street. Willie especially liked Dan Gardiner the clown and Mad'lle Elouise the child [horseback] rider.

November 9th it was cold and windy and as both Willie and Tad had colds, Lincoln said they could not go to the troop review that was being held on the Long Bridge. The boys were not to be deterred. Along with Bud and Holly they snuck out of the Mansion. They had some money left over from their circus last summer so they hired a rickety mule-pulled cart driven by a small, grinning Black boy whom Willie paid twenty-five cents. Each of the boys held a battered sword and followed the line of soldiers. When Lincoln spotted them he looked surprised at first then laughed, but said, "You boys go on home now." Which they dutifully did.

On November 11th in the evening after dark some 2,000 men of Louis Blenker's Division (Louis Blenker May 12, 1812 - October 31, 1863) marched by the Mansion carrying torches honoring General McClellan's promotion to Command of the Armies of the Union. It lit up the whole town.

Willie and Bud went with Lincoln, Secretary Seward and John Hay to General McClellan's house. They waited in the parlor and when McClellan finally came home he ignored them and went to bed. Secretary Seward and Hay were mad but Abe said, "Come, let us go home." Willie asked, "Father, aren't you mad?" Lincoln replied, "No, son, he must have been very tired." Lincoln was always like that thinking of other's feelings. Willie wanted to be like that and usually was. He remembered how kind the General and Mrs. McClellan had been to him and the other boys and knowing the war was on his mind.

Julie had not been to the Mansion for a week and Bud told Willie she had a bad cold and cough but it's slowly getting better. Willie said he would pray for her.

Tad is not doing well for Mr. Williamson and runs away with Mrs. Williamson's books to play rather than sit and study. However, Willie thinks it's not completely Tad's fault. He has a problem concentrating [Attention Deficit Disorder?] and a speech impediment [possibly a cleft palate] that makes it difficult for people to understand him even Mr. Williamson at first and Tad gets frustrated easily.

They all went to see the Grand Review of Troops at Balls X Roads six miles from the river in Virginia. Abe said there were 75,000 men of 80 regiments of infantry, seven of cavalry and 20 batteries of artillery, or pieces. To Willie it seemed the line of troops would never end.

November 23rd Willie and Tad got to stay up late that night to see Hermann (1816 - 1887) the Prestidigitateur [magician] perform his show at the Mansion. Mary Lincoln had invited him to come after his performance at the National Theatre to entertain her guests. Abe, Willie and Tad thought he was very good and both boys wanted to try some of the tricks themselves. However, that morning Willie had some bad news. His Sunday School teacher at New York Avenue Presbyterian Church, Miss *Mattie Waller had died suddenly the day before. She was a great teacher and made the Bible stories and scripture more interesting.

*Her name was actually Harriet Almira "Hattie" Waller (1842 - November 22, 1861). She was born in Ireland.

A Miss Dunham took over Willie's Sunday School Class. She seemed nice but Willie missed Miss Waller. Willie joined the Youth Missionary Society which sponsored missionaries to China. Willie hoped it would turn some of those people to Christ.

Willie and Tad went over to the Taft's to go with Bud, Holly and Mrs. Taft to see General McClellan's review of the Regulars that was held a little east of the Capitol.

November 28th, Thanksgiving. Lincoln said he hoped to persuade Congress to pass a bill designating the last Thursday in November as the Official Day of Thanksgiving and make it a national holiday but that might have to wait till the war was over.

Tad liked to do a lot of pranks around the Mansion and Willie confessed that sometimes he liked to also. In an anteroom of Lincoln's office there was a marble bust of John Forsythe (October 22, 1780 - October 21, 1841) the former Secretary of State from 1834 -1841 and Willie always felt he was "staring" at him so Willie couldn't resist taking a pencil and drawing a beard and goatee on his face.

December 2nd Bud came to the Mansion and was excited at the possibility of finally getting the place of page in he House of Representatives. He was certainly eligible since he turned 14 last January 15th. Bud never heard anything about his application submitted last July with Lincoln's recommendation.

The weather was mild in Washington and Willie and Tad missed the snow, sledding, skating and snowball fights like they had back in Springfield. Bud and Holly said they hadn't seen a snowstorm since they moved to Washington from upstate [Lyons] New York in April 1859; just occasional wet snows that only amounted to an inch or two and soon melted. So the boys decided to have their own "snowstorm." They went to the Mansion attic where they had their circus and found boxes of old namecards from previous Mansion functions over the years, balled them up and threw them up in the air and stuffed them down each other's blouses and pants pretending they were real snow. They made a "sleigh" using an old chair with a missing seat that they filled with an old copy of the *Congressional Directory* and pushed each other around. Willie and his companions had great imaginations and utilized with great delight whatever was available to enhance their play unlike most kids today who are deluged with a myriad of toys and electronic devices. .

They heard a lot of firing from across the river and Mary Lincoln was worried it was the rebels coming but Abe assured her and the boys it was just Union troops practicing shooting off munitions at the forts. Lincoln said that the force across the river is now 200,000 men and about 50,000 on this side. Washington is well-protected but very crowded and sanitation and disease are major concerns.

December 9th it was warm. The boys played outside but it was very muddy. A group of Indians from the West visited Lincoln. They were gaily dressed in headdresses of many colors and some wore necklaces of claws and beads with clothes of animal skins and moccasins.

The next day, December 10th it was very warm for December unlike Springfield. Bud, Holly and Julie came to the Mansion in the afternoon. Willie and Bud went over to the Conservatory so But could pick out a water lily from the aquarium to take home. Bud said little Willie is quite sick with a tummy ache.

December 17th the first big levee [reception] of the season was held that evening in the Mansion. Willie and Tad ran around looking at all the gentlemen in their fancy suits, soldiers in their smart, blue uniforms, ladies in their fine gowns and snuck bon-bons from the table.

They heard heavy guns from across the river. Lincoln said some in the distance might be rebel guns at Centreville.

December 21st, 1861, the winter solstice, Willie Lincoln turned eleven. He would not know it would be his last on this earthly plain before his transition into the Great Mystery.

Bud, Holly and little Willie came to his birthday party. Julie had been invited but was with one of her beaus. During the day different people came up to Willie to shake his hand and said things like this, "He was intellectually and empathically developed far beyond his age." Willie didn't know but guessed he did come to understand things and people better than most boys his age except Bud. Bud understood a lot and would soon be fifteen. Willie wished than sometimes he *didn't* understand because he couldn't *change* things; like Ellsworth and Baker getting killed and all the others and all the sickness. Lincoln used a big word to describe what Willie meant; "predestination." People said Willie could grow up to be a great writer, clergyman or statesman, maybe even president like his father. Willie had thought of becoming a teacher or preacher but right then he was just enjoying being a boy playing with his brother and companions.

December 24th, Christmas Eve, after a dinner with friends and family, the Lincolns sat around the marble fireplace to listen to Abe read *A Visit From St. Nicholas* as was their custom back in Springfield.

December 25th, Christmas Day, Bob was home and it was great to have the whole family reunited for the holiday. When Willie came downstairs in the morning and looked at his stocking hanging from the fireplace it was unusually bulging and drooping down. Excitedly he took it down and found that in addition to the nuts, candy and firecrackers in it were two bright new shiny passenger cars from the B & O Railroad for his train. Willie and Tad also received magic lanterns and planned a show for the new year. In the afternoon Willie and Tad went over to the Taft's and had fun putting off firecrackers and cap pistols with the boys. They stayed for dinner with the Taft's at 4 o'clock.

The next day, December 26th, one of the Army's huge horse corrals at 21st and D Streets that included ten long pine-sheds caught fire. Some 150 - 230 horses died and a thousand others that were cut loose stampeded thought the city in a panic. The city smelt like burnt horse-flesh added to the general stink of the canal and would for days to come.

Bud and Holly came to the Mansion and Mary Lincoln had them stay for dinner. Abe took time to tell the boys new stories and wrestle.

December 31st, 1861. Bud came over that evening to help Willie and Tad set up their magic lantern show. Abe came down and watched it for awhile. Since Willie was now eleven Lincoln let him stay up till midnight to toast in the new year. Tad fussed that he was going to stay up too and Abe said OK but Tad was out like a light by 10 o'clock. At the stroke of midnight they all sipped from fruit punch and sang "Auld Lang Sine." Cannons, pistols and firecrackers were heard all over the city in celebration.

January 1, 1862, New Year's Day Willie got up at 9 o'clock and went outside to find the weather balmy, in the 60s, before the guests arrived for the big Mansion reception and party. By 10 0'clock there were big lines on the lawn waiting to shake hands with the president who shook so many his hands were swollen. Willie went up and greeted Mr. Seth Kinnan (September 29, 1815 - February 24, 1888), the California woodsman who dressed in buckskins and came to every reception when he was in town. He told Willie and Tad exciting stories of the frontier, mountains, gold prospectors, Mexicans and Indians that reminded the boys of their past heroes like Daniel Boone [a distant relative of theirs], Jim Bowie, Davy Crockett and others who were killed defending the Alamo. Later Willie and Tad went over to the Taft's for dinner and brought back Bud and Holly to the Mansion for an overnight stay.

January 2nd Willie and Tad went over to the Taft's and were invited to stay for dinner after which they brought Bud, Holly and little Willie back to the Mansion for their magic lantern show. Abe, of course, got a free ticket. Everyone else had to pay a nickel. Lincoln looked on with glee and the boys had their magic lanterns [devices having an enclosed lamp and lens-like opening formerly used for projecting images mounted on paper] set-up around the grounds and set off firecrackers. Some of the servants who hadn't heard about the boys continued New Year's celebration came running when they heard the firecrackers thinking they were gunshots and the Mansion was being attacked. It was great fun and Lincoln thought it was too, laughing at the panicky servants but he assured them all was well.

January 5th brought with it a dramatic drop in temperature down to 14 degrees, typical of Washington's very changeable winter weather. The boys heard that one Pvt. Michael Lanahan was to be hanged the next day [January 6, 1862. It was the first military execution in Washington during the war] on a scaffold newly built between O and P Streets on the Commons and wanted to go but Lincoln said it was not appropriate for such young eyes as theirs. Willie asked what Lanahan had done to get hanged and Lincoln said he killed his sergeant [Sgt. Joseph Brennan, (? - October 28, 1861) Company A, 2nd U.S. Army, Sgt. of the Guard at Georgetown] which brought chills down Willie's spine.

Lincoln took Willie, Tad and the Taft boys along with him to General McClellan's house. The general was out riding. He had been sick but is much better. Abe said there were over 400 cases of small pox in the city. Bud said that his father told him he is going to have the whole family vaccinated again. Lincoln said that Willie and Tad would be too. Tad yelled, "I don't want no more needles!" Willie told him it's better than getting the pox and dying.

January 7th it snowed a little, about two inches, and Willie Tad, Bud and Holly had snowball battles on the Mansion lawn. They had a good time till the afternoon when it melted and they got wet.

January 9th brought very changeable weather; way below freezing yesterday and raining this day. Willie took his writing paper and pencils and went over to the Taft's where he wrote poems, RR timetables and other memoranda while sitting next to Bud who showed quite a talent for drawing and painting with water colors and draws wonderful houses, steamboats and soldiers.

January 10th it was warm. Holly and little Willie were over at the Mansion for tutoring with Mr. Williamson. All the boys practice reading, writing, spelling and ciphering. Willie said his letters to Henry Remann are getting better and others are getting better but he still needs to work on his punctuation. Holly said that Bud also takes Latin lessons. Tad tries to learn but soon gets frustrated and runs out. He can't seem to pay attention very long. Abe says he'll learn in due time. Willie loved to learn with Mr. Williamson and in Sunday School. That afternoon Dr. Robert King Stone (December 11, 1822 - April 23, 1872), the Lincoln family physician in Washington, came and vaccinated Willie and Tad against small pox [an early, often ineffective vaccine that sometimes caused a varioloid or allergic reaction that was fatal]. Tad squealed like a stuck pig. Willie winced at the needle but it was over quickly and they got candy. Very foggy in the evening.

January 11th was warm and pleasant. Willie Tad and the Taft boys went up to the Mansion roof which is copper, flat and had a high stone balustrade all around and set up a fort-combination cabin that the boys called the "Ship of State" or, rather the "Quarter Deck." They borrowed Lincoln's spyglass and reported all strange sails on the river and objects on the Virginia shore. Tad said some boats on the river were pirates but Willie told him he didn't think pirates came that far inland. They raised and lowered a U.S. flag with due ceremony. Abe is Commodore, the Cabinet are officers but they sail the Ship of State. They had a rare [exceptionally fun] time and "sank" two secesch invaders with their long-range "guns." Julie came up to the roof wanting the scissors they had borrowed and she was received at the "side" with

Naval etiquette. They showed her the Confederate flag at Munson's Hill clearly visible through the spyglass.

January 12th Willie had developed a cold.

January 13th Bud went to the Mansion to see how Willie was feeling. Willie was feeling better. Bud said his father's birthday is today. He is 56 and his (Bud's) is two days from now on the 15th and he'll be 15 and wanted Willie and Tad to come to his party at 3 o'clock. Lincoln appointed Edward M. Stanton of Pennsylvania as Secretary of War to replace Simon Cameron who also had been from Pennsylvania and was sent to be Minister to Russia succeeding Cassius Clay who will become a general in the Army.

January 14th it snowed and Willie wanted to go out but Mary Lincoln said he should stay in as he was not completely over his cold and tomorrow was Bud's birthday and Willie wanted to be well for that.

January 15th the weather turned really cold again and it was sleeting. Willie and Tad went to Bud's birthday party. There was chocolate cake, vanilla ice cream, various other treats and they played games. Bud was very happy with his new set of water colors. Lincoln said that small pox and typhoid were both prevailing among the people and soldiers to a great extent.

January 16th it got colder again and the snow and sleet that had melted turned the streets to ice. Willie, Tad and the Taft boys went skating. Willie and Tad had dinner at the Taft's and Mary Lincoln sent along a request that Bud and Holly sleep over at the Mansion and they did.

January 17th. Willie can't seem to get used to the changeable weather. He wished it would just stay *cold* and snow every day like back in Springfield. The ice melted and all the roads were muddy and slushy again. Willie went with Bud and Mr. Taft to get Bud a new pair of rubbers at a store on 7th Street. Holly had a bad cold. Julie had been revaccinated and the rest of the Taft's soon would be. Small pox was rampant.

January 18th Bob came home from Cambridge (Harvard) to spend his vacation (winter break) and Bud stayed for dinner. Holly is till sick.

January 19th it rained all day. Willie went to Sunday School but stayed in the rest of the day and played trains with Tad and Old Edward [McManus the doorkeeper] and Abe when he had a free moment.

January 20th was another rainy day. Small pox is very bad among the soldiers down by the river but also among people not far from the Mansion down 9th Street. Willie saw a small pox ambulance with the yellow flag on it go down Pennsylvania Avenue. Everyone is much alarmed. Lincoln said Dr. Stone will be at the Mansion to revaccinate the boys tomorrow. Tad howled when he heard that.

January 21st it rained again. Dr. Stone came about 10 o'clock and revaccinated Willie and Tad. Tad fussed, fumed and cried.

January 22nd Lincoln took the boys out to the grounds south of the Mansion to see a demonstration of Shorts and Smiths Greek Fire Bomb set off. Lincoln said it was a great success. He was very interested in new weapons to fight the secesch. The fire bomb looked like one big firecracker going off.

Saturday, January 25th someone one gave Willie a *pony. Willie adored the pony and from that day on rode it daily regardless of the changeable weather and his mother's admonitions.

*Possibly Lincoln family friend Orville Hickman or Secretary Seward who had given the Lincolns kittens and other pets.

January 26th Willie and Tad went to Sunday School and church with Mr. Taft, Julie and the boys and Willie told them about his new pony and invited Bud and Holly to come and see the pony after church but they couldn't come that day but would the next day. Willie and Tad took turns riding the pony in the afternoon.

The next day, January 27th, Bud, Holly and little Willie came to the Mansion and they all rode Willie's pony.

January 28th after three nice days it rained all day. Mary Lincoln had another big levee that evening. Julie came with friends. She looked very smart.

January 29th it rained in the morning but cleared by afternoon. Bud and Holly came to the Mansion and they had a great time riding Willie's pony.

January 30th rain again. Bud came in the afternoon and they rode Willie's pony though Mary Lincoln wasn't pleased that they went riding in that weather. After they were done riding they went over to the Taft's and Mrs. Taft noticed their feet were wet and made them dry them off. Dr. Barnes (Norman D. Barnes 1830 - April 18, 1885) of the 27th New York Volunteers happened to be calling on the Taft's that day and Mrs. Taft asked him to give Willie and Tad a ride back to the Mansion in his ambulance which was exciting.

January 31st was cloudy but at least no rain and Willie rode his pony most of the afternoon. They both got pretty muddy and Mary Lincoln said that they were running out of clean pants for Willie and it was driving the washer servants crazy.

February 1st Willie awoke to find the ground covered with snow in the morning that melted by afternoon. Bud didn't come to the Mansion as he had a severe cold.

February 2nd Mary Lincoln didn't let Willie go to church as he had too come down with a severe cold.

February 4th Willie wanted to ride his pony but his cold was worse and his mother made him sit by the fireplace all day wrapped in blankets.

February 5th Willie was put to bed in the Prince of Wales Room named in honor of the Prince of Wales who had stayed there during the Buchanan administration. It was Mary Lincoln's favorite room that she had lavishly decorated. Willie had a bad headache, fever, chest pain and found it hard to breathe. His mother and Mrs. Keckly put cold compresses on his forehead to try and bring the fever down. Mary summoned Dr. Stone who came to see Willie in the afternoon. He said he thought Willie had bilious fever [an abnormal, excess secretion of bile from the liver] and gave instructions to Aunt Mary (Mary Dines 1820 -?) to give the boy Peruvian bark, calomel [a white tasteless powder used chiefly as a purgative] and jalap [a light yellowish powder derived from the morning glory plant family used chiefly as a purgative] at half-hour intervals when he was awake and his mother is also to give Willie beef tea, blackberry cordial and Mrs. Leslie's (Eliza Leslie - November 15, 1787 - January 1, 1858) bland puddings but none of those remedies seem to help much. That evening Mrs. Lincoln had the first Mansion ball downstairs. Willie could hear the band and wished he could go down. Abe and Mary frequently came up from the ball to see Willie.

February 6th steady rain and sleet.

February 7th Abe sat with Willie most of the day.

February 8th the head nurse said the papers reported that Willie had typhoid fever.

February 10th Willie felt better and was able to sit in the chair next to the bed and write. Mrs. Keckly came in and saw Willie and said, "Land sakes, child, what are you doing out of bed? You know you need your rest," Tad is also sick.

February 11th Lincoln sat with both boys most of the day.

February 12th Abraham Lincoln was 53. Willie was well enough to sit up and have a piece of his father's birthday cake. Abe sat with Willie a long time. Willie thought his father looked exhausted. He worries about the war, Willie and Tad too much. Abe told Willie that the Union troops beat the secesch in North Carolina and captured Roanoke Island and Fort Henry, Tennessee. Lincoln said other than Willie and Tad getting well it was the best birthday present he could ask for.

February 13th Mary Lincoln exclaimed worriedly, "The fever lingers. Willie is particularly weak." Abe asked, " What does Dr. Stone say?" Mary replied, "He said this ague [a malarial-like fever characterized by regular returning paroxysms, marked by successive cold, hot and sweating fits] is a new one, not like the others."

February 14th Willie said that Bud had not been to the Mansion since he (Willie) got sick. Willie asked his father to see if Bud could come and stay with him.

February 15th. Snowfall. Lincoln came into Willie's room and said there was to be a great battle at Fort Donelson, Tennessee. Bud came in the afternoon and Willie was very glad to see him. They've always had a special understanding and affection for each other. Bud sat by the bed and held Willie's hand. This simple gesture made Willie feel better just knowing Bud was holding his hand.

February 16th Bud came up to the sick room after tutoring and skipped dinner to sit with Willie. Willie told him he should eat but Bud said he didn't have an appetite if Willie didn't. Mrs. Keckly whispered sadly and softly to herself, "Willie is fading away."

February 17th Mary Lincoln and Bud were with Willie almost all day. Lincoln came when he could. Abe came again late that evening and found Bud still there fast asleep in the chair by Willie's bed. Lincoln woke him and told him he ought to go to bed in the boys' room, but Bud said, "If I go he will call for me later." When Willie woke up Bud was gone. Abe had carried him to bed. Bud had stayed over at the Mansion the last two nights.

February 18th Dr. Gurley, (Phineas D. Gurley November 12, 1816 - September 30, 1868), pastor of the New York Ave. Presbyterian Church, came in the morning and Willie, *who knew he was dying,* asked the pastor to take the five dollars that were in Willie's bank on the mantel and please send them to the missionaries in China for him. Dying, he still thought of others before himself.

February 19th rain pelted down on the window of the Prince of Wales room. Mrs. Keckly and Bud stayed with Willie that evening. Mary Lincoln touched Willie's face that is very hot with fever. Cold compresses no longer helped. Mary Lincoln said, "The crisis should come." Mrs. Keckly said, "It's never the same with this kind of fever that the doctor said was *new* to him." Mary Lincoln replied, "There is no difference." Abe came in and rested his big hand on Willie's face very gently and said, "He is no worse; that is something." But Willie knew he was.

Thursday, February 20th, 1862. Mary Lincoln's held Willie's hand.

Mrs. Keckly stood beside her. Dr. Stone tried to get Willie to take some medicine but he was too weary and weak to open his mouth Lincoln came in the room and as he approached the bed Willie opened his eyes and tried to speak but couldn't. The doctor lifted Willie's head and managed to get some medicine down his throat. Willie nodded and swallowed. About 5 o'clock Bud is holding Willie's hand and Mary Lincoln came into the room. She asked Bud if Willie had spoken. Bud shook his head and said, "But he recognizes me sometimes. He squeezes my hand a little." A few minutes later Bud cried out, "His hand isn't holding mine anymore!" Mrs. Keckly said through tears, "Willie's blue eyes have closed forever." Bud and Mary Lincoln wept uncontrollably. The president cries out, "My boy is gone! He is really gone! He was too good for this earth! God has called him home! I know he is better off in Heaven, but we loved him so! It is hard! It is hard to have him die!"

The Harvester came for this flower in the morning of life before the impure spirit of the world tarnished his innocence and he was carried to Paradise in the arms of the Angels.

- Speur Antoine de Jesus

Willie about age 4 Springfield 1855

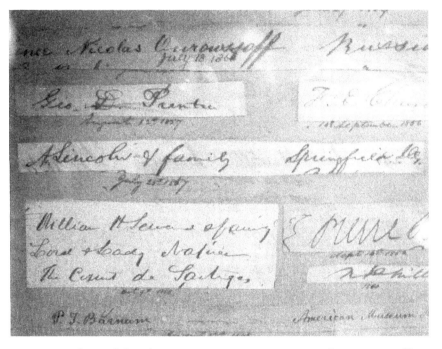

A. Lincoln and family signature on guest register of Niagara Falls Museum July 1857.

Daguerreotype of Willie and lock of his hair 1859.

Mary (Todd) Lincoln's invitation to Willie's 9th birthday party.

Willie, age 9 Springfield 1859

Dr. William S. Wallace Willie's namesake, uncle and family doctor originally from Lancaster Pennsylvania.

Henry Christian Remann Willie's best friend in Springfield.

Grave stone of Edward "Eddie" Rathbun and brother James Miner Rathbun, Wood Lawn Cemetery, Wellsville, NY

Fido the Lincoln family dog 1861.

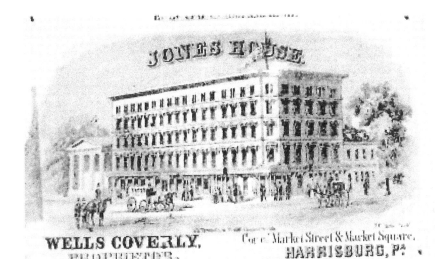

JONES HOUSE

WELLS COVERLY, PROPRIETOR.

Cor. of Market Street & Market Square, HARRISBURG, PA.

IT WAS AT THE JONES HOUSE THAT ABRAHAM LINCOLN STOPPED WHEN HE WAS ON HIS WAY TO WASHINGTON TO BE INAUGURATED FOR PRESIDENT OF THE UNITED STATES IN 1861.

GEN. GEORGE WASHINGTON WAS A GUEST HERE ON OCT 3, 1794 ON HIS WAY TO THE WHISKEY INSURRECTION.

IN 1859 THE LATE KING EDWARD OF ENGLAND, THEN THE PRINCE OF WALES WAS ENTERTAINED HERE. IT WAS ALSO THE SCENE OF MANY POLITICAL BATTLES.

Jones House Hotel, Harrisburg, PA where Willie, Tad & Mary (Todd) Lincoln stayed the night of February 23, 1861.

Elizabeth Keckly

Horatio "Bud" Nelson Taft & Halsey "Holly" Cook Taft Willie & Tad's best friends in Washington 1861.

Julia Taft Bud & Holly's older sister 1861.

PROGRAME.

I PART.

Hail Columbia . . . . Troupe

Star Spangled banner . . - Billy Sanders . Tad Lincoln

Home, Sweet Home . . Joe Corkhead . . Bud Taft

. . J. King . Willie Lincoln

. . C. Donelson . Holly Taft

II. PART.

Banjo Solo . . . Billy Sanders & Joe Corkhead

Champion Dance . . . Billy Sanders

I am going & I am gone . John Gualld & Joe Corkhead

STOCKS UP & STOCKS DOWN

Joe Corkhead, Billy Sanders & J. K.

The STEAM ARM.

III. PART

TO
Conclude with

THE BLACK STATUE . Tad, Lincoln

admission . . . . 5 Cents

J. King . . . . . proprieter.

Willie's Programme

Colonel Elmer E. Ellsworth 1861.

Colonel Edward D. Baker 1861

Abraham Lincoln 1861

Willie age 10 with Uncle Lockwood Todd's walking stick Brady Studio, Washington April 1861

Willie, Tad & Uncle Lockwood Todd Brady's Studio

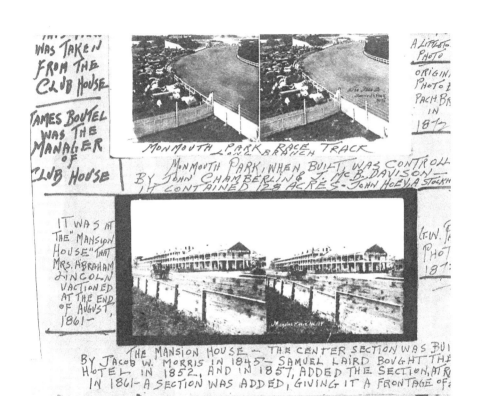

*Mansion House, Long Branch, NJ where Willie Tad, Robert & Mary
(Todd) Lincoln vacationed August 19-24, 1861*

PRESIDENT LINCOLN, TAD AND WILLIE IN FRONT OF THE MARBLE FIREPLACE IN THE WHITE HOUSE, WASHINGTON, D.C. 1861.

Abe, Willie & Tad Christmas 1861, White House.

Prince of Wales Room in White House where Willie died Feb. 20, 1862

William Thomas Carroll Tomb, Oak Hill Cemetery, Georgetown
Where Willie lay from February 24, 1862 to April 20, 1865.

Lincoln and Willie's flower-draped coffins resting in temporary vault
Oak Ridge Cemetery, Springfield, May 5, 1865

Willie & Eddie's crypt Lincoln Tomb, Springfield.

General Andrew Christy Porter, Harrisburg Cemetery.

Willie's Gone To Heaven

Little Willie's gone to heaven,
    Praise the Lord!
All his sins are forgiven,
    Praise the Lord!

Little Willie murmured never
    Praise the Lord!
Willie's soul will live forever,
    Praise the Lord!

In departing he was cheerful,
    Praise the Lord!
He was hopeful, never fearful,
    Praise the Lord!

All the light on him has broken,
    Praise the Lord!
That from Christ was kindly spoken,
    Praise the Lord!

Joyful let your voices rise
    Do not come with tearful eyes,
Willie's dwelling in the skies,
    Willie's gone to heaven.

- Stephen Foster (1863)

POSTSCRIPT

FEBRUARY 20, 1862 about 5:10 p.m. Mrs. Keckly washed Willie and laid him out on the bed.

February 23rd in the Green Room of the Mansion Willie is lying in his coffin. His soft brown hair with blond highlights is parted in the middle over his pale forehead. He looked as if he was sleeping. He is attired in the usual type of clothing worn for everyday; a plain brown suit of clothes that consisted of pants, jacket, white stockings and low cut shoes. The white shirt collar was tuned down over the jacket and the cuffs were turned back over the sleeves. A sheet of white crepe covered the sides of his metallic coffin which gave the appearance of being rosewood. On his left breast had been laid the greenish-yellow flowers of the mignonette. He was tucked beneath a blanket of white camellias and held in one hand a bouquet of read and white camellias. The shades and curtains of the green room were drawn shut and candlelight illuminated Willie's face, the face of an angel in repose. All the mirrors in the Mansion were draped in black crepe for mourning. Senator and Mrs. Orville Browning received mourners for the family, summoning other friends to sit by the coffin. Neither the president nor Mrs. Lincoln had the strength to join the vigil.

Monday, February 24th the funeral was held at 2 p. m. in the East Room. All the government offices in Washington were shut down. The first time that had ever happened except for the death of a president. Willie's coffin, now closed, was left in the Green Room probably to ease the ordeal of the president who attended the funeral only with great difficulty. On the lid of the coffin was a square silver plaque with Willie's name and dates of his birth and death. Robert Lincoln who had come down from Harvard for the funeral and the Lincolns went alone into the Green Room, locked the door and sat with Willie till it was time for the service. The bouquet of camellias that Willie had held in his hand was saved for Mrs. Lincoln who was now so overcome with paroxysms of grief that she could not attend the service and poor Bud was so overcome that he fainted and had to be carried from the room and was ill for several days afterwards. Then the coffin was closed and carried from the Green Room to the hearse by six young pallbearers from Willie's Sunday School Class wearing a yard of white silk with long ends tied around their hats and wreathes of flowers on their arms. The hearse was pulled by two white horses but black horses drew the barouche in which the president and Bob sat. They rode through the flooded, debris-filled streets, remnants of the terrific storm that overnight had torn roofs off houses, knocked down trees, chimneys, steeples, slashed flags and crepe, broke skylights of the Library of Congress and Potomac River waves washed over the Long Bridge. Although the president was not religious in the traditional sense (but very spiritual), and was more of a fatalist he, said later a few days after Willie's death it was symbolic that there should be a big storm and then a great calm and sunshine breaking through when the funeral party reached Oak Hill Cemetery in Georgetown and the beautiful little red stone chapel with blue stained-glass windows. "It was like a resurrection scene," Lincoln exclaimed. Some verses of scripture were read and Willie's coffin rested temporarily there till it was moved to a crypt in the family vault of William Thomas Carroll (March 2, 1802 - July 13, 1863), Clerk of the Supreme Court, who had sworn the president in at his inauguration and was a close family friend. Mr. Carroll had graciously offered the use of a crypt when the president expressed the fact the he wanted to *keep Willie close* and not be sent home to Springfield at that time. Mr. Carroll himself had lost two young sons (William Thomas Carroll, Jr. July 10, 1833 - January 19, 1857) and (Howard Carroll January 28, 1852 - February 21, 1857), to death in the same year and certainly empathized with the president in his grief.

February 25th and for a few days afterwards, the president purportedly visited the Carroll vault and had Willie's coffin taken out of the crypt and moved outside of the vault [the tiled floor was too narrow to fit Abe and Willie's coffin] and opened so he could once more gaze on the countenance of his beloved son. In 2008 when I visited the vault and peered through the thick wrought iron door I could see what appeared to be drag marks the width of a small coffin on the floor leading from the empty crypt, the last one on the far right bottom row. The Carroll vault is the very last one high up at the extreme far reaches of the grounds at the top of an almost perpendicular hillside that descends to Rock Creek below. The rapid, gurgling water of the creek made a pleasant sound and the trees stood as sentinels guarding against the winter sky. It was a beautiful and peaceful spot.

February 26th Mary Lincoln visited Rev. Phineas D. Gurley's office in the New York Presbyterian Church and gave Willie's savings of five dollars to the Reverend to be sent to the missionaries in China. Willie's last request was honored.

March 8th Lincoln has some of Willie's small toys on his desk in his office and fireplace mantel. Above the mantel was a painting of Illinois that Willie had done.

March 30th Mary Lincoln filled up a trunk with things she wanted sent back to Springfield. In it Tad sent two toy train cars that had belonged to Willie to *Edward Lewis Baker, Jr. (October 27, 1858 - February 22, 1923), who was just three at the time and was a grandson of Mrs. Ninian W. Edwards (Elizabeth Porter Todd Edwards November 13, 1813 - February 22, 1888), Mary Lincoln's sister. Tad could not bear to play with them again. Mary Lincoln wrote to Mrs. Taft asking to keep the boys from coming to the Mansion anymore because it made Mary feel worse to see them. Sadly, never again would Tad have the companionship of Bud, Holly or little Willie Taft.

*Efforts to track down descendants of Edward Lewis Baker, Jr., who may have kept Willie's train cars, were unsuccessful.

August 26th Mary Lincoln dreams (but *believes* she is actually seeing and talking to him) of Willie that he is standing at the foot of her bed with the same sweet adorable smile he had in life. According to Mary, Willie appears some nights alone and others with his brother Eddie and Uncle Alec (Confederate Captain Alexander H. Todd February 15, 1839 - August 5, 1862), Mary's half brother who had been recently killed at the Battle of Baton Rouge. Mary believes that sleep and death are allies and the dead contact the living through dreams. Mary attended séances where charlatans preyed on her grief faking messages from Willie.

November 18, 1863 Lincoln gives his famous Gettysburg Address near the battlefield in Gettysburg, Pennsylvania. His wore a black crepe band around his stove pipe hat. When asked what it was for he replied, "It is memory of my dead son Willie."

January 27, 1864 Mary Lincoln held a Saturday reception in the Mansion. Julia Taft had returned to Washington for the first time since Willie's death. Mary greeted her affectionately and asked about her mother and all the family. But when Tad came in the room and saw Julia he threw himself down on the floor in the midst of the guests kicking and screaming until he had to be carried out. Mrs. Lincoln said to Julia, "You must excuse him, Julia, you know what he remembers."

February 10, 1864 a terrible fire burned down the Mansion stables that housed Willie's pony as well as Tad's and the president's and secretaries' horses. Lincoln had rushed out hurtling a hedgerow to try and save the animals but the building was engulfed in flames. Lincoln returned inside the Mansion and stood looking out the window and weeping. Tad said to a bystander that his father is crying because Willie's pony was in there and he remembered how much Willie loved that pony and all the anguish of Willie's suffering and death was brought back.

April 15, 1865, ten minutes after 7 a.m. Abraham Lincoln dies from the head wound fired by assassin John Wilkes Booth the evening before.

April 20, 1865, Oak Hill Cemetery, Georgetown, William Thomas Carroll vault. The caretaker unlocked the heavy, ornate, iron door and two workmen carefully remove the coffin of Willie Lincoln from the crypt where it had rested for over three years, carried it down the path to the cemetery road and loaded it on to a wagon that brought it to the B & O Station and placed it on to the funeral car where Lincoln's coffin joined him the next day. They placed Willie's metallic coffin in a new black walnut coffin. The workmen were paid ten dollars.

April 21, 1865 the funeral car began its 1,600 mile long, sad journey home to Springfield.

April 28, 1865 Columbus, Ohio. At that stop of the funeral train two children brought to the funeral car a bunch of violets and daffodils arranged in a wreath which they had gathered from a field. Not thinking it was quite right that all the flowers should be placed on the coffin of the president they wanted that their offering should be placed on Willie's coffin which was done. The flowers and note accompanying them was given to Mrs. Lincoln who was deeply affected by the incident, especially by the note that read:

> *We knew everyone would give Mr. Lincoln flowers*
> *so we made this wreath for little Willie's coffin.*
> *We thought he might be lonely.*

May 4th, 1865, Oak Ridge Cemetery, Springfield, Illinois. Willie's and the president's coffins were placed in a receiving vault till a permanent one could be built. Many speeches and tributes were given and songs sung, One in particular resonated through the crowd of mourners:

Lord, obediently we will go,
Gladly leaving all below;
Only thou our leader be,
And we shall follow Thee.

December 21, 1865, Oak Ridge Cemetery. Mrs. Lincoln and Robert Lincoln have been informed that the coffins of the president, Willie and Edward "Eddie" Baker Lincoln [who had died February 1, 1850 of tuberculosis and had been interred in Hutchinson's Cemetery in Springfield, exhumed December 13th and placed in the receiving vault with the president and Willie] were to be removed from the receiving vault to a temporary underground vault near the construction site of the permanent monument. Mrs. Lincoln chose 3 p.m. for her to be present for the move. A sudden indisposition came over her and she did not attend. Since that, day, December 21, 1865, would have been Willie's 15th birthday and seeing the coffins of her husband and two of her children it was certainly understandable that she became indisposed as it would have been too painful a scene and on Willie's birthday.

July 15, 1871 Thomas "Tad" Lincoln died of "dropsy of the chest" [probably pleurisy] in a Chicago hotel where he and Mary Lincoln had been staying after their return from Europe.

September 19, 1871 the coffins of Lincoln, Willie, Eddie are removed from the temporary underground vault and placed in crypts (Willie and Eddie in one) in the nearly completed permanent monument.

July 16, 1882 at the home of Mrs. Edward's Mrs. Lincoln's sister in Springfield, Mary Lincoln died, almost to the date 11 years later when Tad died.

Now, except for Robert Lincoln who would live into the 20th century, the little family *all belong to the ages...together!*

Over the years servants, White House staff and guests who slept in the Prince of Wales Room [now called the Lincoln bedroom although he never slept there] in the ornate bed that Willie died in, or ventured down to the end of the hall near that room have reported seeing a young boy dressed in 1860s period clothing. During President Grant's administrations [1869-1872, 1873-1877] according to *New York Times* Pulitzer Prize winning reporter and journalist Arthur Krock (November 16, 1886 - April 12, 1974), a boy whom the servants and staff recognized as the apparition of little Willie Lincoln "materialized" before their eyes. The last known report was in a letter from Major Archibald Willingham Butt (September 26, 1864 - April 15, 1912), the aide-de-camp to President William Howard Taft to his sister July 26, 1911 stating that White House housekeeper Elizabeth Ann (Nunn) Jaffray (December 26, 1860 - May 2, 1934) from 1909 - 1926 that she and other staff had seen and felt the ghost of a little boy on several occasions.

O lost and by the Time grieved,
Willie, return again!

Obituary, Notice of Embalming, Funeral, Eulogies, Tributes and Letters of Sympathy for Willie

Obituary - *Washington Evening Star*, February 21, 1862

The public rejoicings at the recent success of the Union army will be clouded by the intelligence of the death of the second son of the President [actually 3ʳᵈ son], and the country will sympathize with the bereaved parents in such a heavy affliction. Willie Lincoln was a boy of unusual intelligence, and was a favorite of all who visited the White House. Some weeks since he was taken sick with an intermittent fever, which soon assumed a typhoid character, and since that time the little sufferer has been gradually sinking. Much of the time his mind has been wandering, and only those parents who have seen a young child a prey to fever and delirium can imagine the anguish of the father and mother as they watched the progress of the disease, without the power to alleviate his sufferings. His condition has been very critical for more than a week, and last Monday his condition was considered almost hopeless. Since Wednesday he has sunk rapidly, and yesterday it was seen that he was dying. He lingered until 5 o'clock in the afternoon when his spirit was released.

Drs. Stone and Hall have attended the deceased and his younger brother since their illness. The latter is yet ill, but it is hoped not dangerously so. The President has, with Mrs. Lincoln, watched by the side of his suffering children for ten days past, and in all that time had scarcely any rest, as in the midst of his domestic affliction the cares of State were upon him.

Willie was a fine looking boy and his intelligence and vivacity made him a favorite with old and young. He was a faithful attendant at Dr. Gurley's church, and the last day he was present there told his tutor that when he attained manhood he wanted to be a school teacher or preacher of the gospel. His exercises in literary composition were very credible for a youth of his age, and he seemed to take great pride in them.

Notice of embalming and Members of the Cabinet and their Families Calling on the president and Mrs. Lincoln. - *Washington Evening Star*, February 22, 1862.

Little Willie Lincoln - It will be a source of gratification to the friends of the President to learn that the remains of the little favorite of the White House have been embalmed by Dr. Charles De Costa Brown (March 3, 1817 - July 12, 1896), assisted by Dr. Joseph R. Alexander (July 6, 1838 - Nov. 15, 1915) and Dr. Charles A. Wood (1825 - 1888),with a new method using zinc chloride which gave the body the appearance of marble. Also present were the family physicians, Dr. James Croudhill Hall (January 10, 1805 - June 7, 1880) and Dr. Robert K. Stone, Senator Browning, Isaac Newton, Esq. (? - March 6, 1901), and others. The embalmment was a complete success, and gave great satisfaction to all present. The body will be deposited in a vault on next Monday, and will eventually moved to Illinois, to be deposited in family burying ground of the President.

By Joint Resolution of Congress, public buildings were not illuminated the night of Washington's birthday February 22 out of respect for the President's family.

Yesterday morning the members of the Cabinet with their families called on the President and Mrs. Lincoln to express their condolence. No others were admitted to the Presidential mansion. The Foreign Ministers, Senators and other leading citizens sent cards of condolence. Senator Browning has entire charge of the funeral arrangements.

Funeral of the President's Son, *National Intelligencer,* Washington, February 25, 1862.

In respect of the funeral ceremonies at the President's mansion yesterday, business was suspended in all governments.

During the morning hours many visitors availed themselves of the opportunity to take a last view of the features of the boy who death has stricken so many hearts. In the East Room the large magnificent mirrors were festooned with mourning drapery. The body of the deceased remained in the "Green Parlor" [Green Room] adjoining.

The coffin that enclosed the remains was metallic, and finished in imitation of rosewood. On a plain silver plate was inscribed "William Wallace Lincoln, born December 21, 1850, died February 20, 1862."

As the large concourse of spectators gazed on the lad, lovely in death, many tears fell on the coffin.

By the hour of two o'clock the East Room was filled with the revered clergy, the mourners, the members of the Cabinet, Foreign Ministers, Senators, and members of the House of Representatives, the Mayor, and citizens in general.

Rev. P. D. Gurley, D.D., of the Presbyterian Church, rose and commenced the services by reading appropriate passages of the Holy Scriptures. This he followed with an appropriate and impressive address, in which he made special reference to the loved one whose departure had saddened so many hearts. The reverend speaker skillfully extended his remarks so as to afford consolation to every sorrowing parent present. When he concluded, the throne of Divine grace was expressed by the Rev. John C. Smith, D.D.

The coffin was removed to the hearse. Six pall bearers followed, viz; Messrs, Ashbury, Pope, Watts, Gurley, Denham and Kerr, and Sabbath School scholars in the same class with the deceased youth. The Rev. Drs. Gurley and Smith, the President accompanied by his eldest son Robert, and Private Secretary Nicolay, the Illinois delegates, Vice President Hamlin (August 27, 1809 - July 4, 1891), Heads of Departments, Major General McClellan, Foreign Ministers, members of Congress and citizens generally,

The solemn procession then moved onward to the beautiful Oak Hill Cemetery on the picturesque heights of Georgetown. On arrival there, the length of the cortege rendered it necessary to extend the route to High Street, thence around the reservoir to the cemetery.

All having alighted another procession was formed, and proceeded to the Cemetery Chapel, where the solemn burial service was repeated by Dr. Gurley, after which the coffin was deposited in a receptacle prepared for it, and susceptible to a ready removal to Illinois.

Contemporary Eulogies, Tributes and Letters of Sympathy for Willie

President Lincoln: - "This is the hardest trial of my life! Why is it? Why is it? My boy is gone! He is really gone! He was too good for this earth! But then God has called him home. I know that he is better off in heaven, but we loved him so! It is hard, hard to have him die!"

During the week of May 5th, 1862 while visiting Fort Monroe in Virginia, the President had a conversation with an Army staff person named Legrand Cannon (November 1, 1815 - November 3, 1900). He asked (after reading the passage from Shakespeare's *King John* [3:3] where

Constance bewails the loss of her child to the king), "Did you ever dream of a lost friend and feel you were having a direct conversation with that friend yet have a consciousness that it was not a reality? Just so I dream of my boy Willie." He was so utterly overcome his great frame shook and bowing down on the table he wept as only such a man in the breaking down of a great sorrow could weep. Later, also, the President who was never a Christian in the traditional sense, had conversations with the clergy about God and the afterlife and said, "I shall go to God with my sorrows."

The President also said that he placed some of Willie's small toys on his office desk, and fireplace mantel, and a picture Willie drew of Illinois over the fireplace and feels his presence. He also said he dreams of Willie almost every night only to wake up in the morning and realize it was only a dream. *Or was it?*

King John [3:3]

And Father Cardinal, I have heard you say
That we shall see and know our friends in heaven;
If that be true I shall see my boy again;
For since the birth of Cain, the first male child,
To him but yesterday suspire,
There was not such a gracious creature born.

But not will canker-sorrow eat my bud
And chase the native beauty from his cheek
And he will look as hollow as a ghost,
As dim and meager as an ague's fit,
And so he'll die, and rising so again,
When I shall meet him again in the court of heaven
I shall not know him; therefore never, never
Must I behold my pretty Arthur [Willie] more.

Grief fills the room up of my absent child,
Lies in his bed, walks up and down with me,
Puts on his pretty looks, repeats his words,
Remembers me of all his gracious parts,
Stuffs out his vacant garments with his form;
Then, have I reason to be fond of grief?
Fare you well; had you such a loss as I,
I could give better comfort than you do.
I will not keep this form upon my head,
When there is such disorder in my wit.

O Lord, My boy, my Arthur [Willie], my fair son!
My life, my joy, my food, my all the world!

Mary Lincoln - May 29, 1862. "We have met with so overwhelming an affliction in the death of our beloved Willie, a being too precious for this earth. All that human skill could do, was done for our sainted boy. I fully believe the severe illness [scarlet fever in June 1860 that he suffered from for nearly a month and can cause damaged heart valves] he passed through, now, nearly almost two years hence, was but a warning to us, that one so pure, was not to remain long here and at the same time he was lent to us a little longer- to try us and wean us from our world, whose chains were fastening around us and when the blow came, it found us so unprepared to meet it. Our home is very beautiful, the grounds around it are enchanting, the world still smiles and pays homage, yet charm is dispelled- everything appears a mockery, the idolized one is not with us, he has fulfilled his mission and we are left desolate. When I think over his short but happy childhood, how much comfort, he always was to me, and how fearfully, I always found my hopes concentrating on so good a boy as he was- when I can bring myself to realize that he has indeed passed away, my question to myself is, 'can life be endured?'"

July 26, 1862 - "In the loss of our idolized boy, we naturally have suffered such intense grief, that a removal from the scene of our misery was found very necessary. Yet in this sweet spot [Soldier's Home] that his bright nature would have so well loved, he is not with us, and the anguish of the thought, offtimes for days overcomes me. How often I felt rebellious and almost believe that our Heavenly Father has forsaken us in removing so lovely a child from us. Yet I know a great sin is committed when we feel thus."

August 26, 1862 - "He comes to me every night, and stands at the foot of the bed with same, sweet adorable smile he always had; he does not always come alone; little Eddie is sometimes with him and twice he has come with our brother Alex. He tells me he loves his Uncle Alec and is with him most of the time. You cannot dream of the comfort this gives me. The thought of my little boy in the immensity, alone, without his mother to direct him, no one to hold his little hand in loving guidance, it nearly broke my heart."

*Underlining is Mary Lincoln's.

December 16, 1862 - "Even for this time until spring each day will be a gloomy anniversary. My precious little Willie is much mourned over, & far more missed (now that we realize that he is gone) then when so fearful a stroke as to be called upon to resign Him, came."

February 21, 1863 - [First anniversary of Willie's death February 20, 1862]. "Only those who have passed through such bereavements, can realise how the heart bleeds at the return, of these anniversaries-our precious lambs, if we could only realise, how far happier they are now then when on earth! Heaven help the sorrowing, and full the land is, of such!'

November 20, 1864 - "Since we were heavily visited by affliction, almost three years since the loss of our darling Willie, with the sensitiveness of heavy sorrow, I have shrank from all communication with those who would most forcible recall my sorrows to my mind. The fairest are most frequently taken from a world of trial for some wise purpose which we cannot understand. Willie, darling boy!, was always the idolized child of the household, so gentle, so meek for a more Heavenly home. We were having <u>so much bliss</u>. Doubtless ere this, our angel boys are reunited for they loved each other so much on earth." [Refers to the death of Edward "Eddie" Rathbun, Jr. 1848 - 1862, Willie's friend in Springfield 1857-59 and son of Mrs. John Shearer who had accompanied, along with her sons, Mary Lincoln, Willie and Tad on vacation to Long Branch New Jersey in August 1861].

June 15, 1865 - "For all your great kindness [refers to Alexander Williamson, Willie's tutor] to my darling boys, may Heaven forever bless you! I am sure my angel boy in Heaven loves you as dearly as ever. He was too pure for earth and God recalled his own."

November 15, 1865 - "I enclose one photograph of my precious sainted Willie. You [Francis Bicknell Carpenter August 6, 1830 - May 23, 1900, artist, who stayed at the White House in 1864 and painted scene of the signing of the Emancipation Proclamation] have doubtless heard how very handsome a boy he was considered- with a pure, gentle nature, always unearthly, & in intellect, far, far beyond his years- when I reflect as I am doing, upon the overwhelming loss of the <u>most</u> idolized boy, and the crushing blow that deprived me of my <u>*all in all*</u> in this life, I wonder that I retain my reason and live."

December 8, 1865 - "I thought you [Carpenter, who also painted a family portrait that included Willie posthumously] would be satisfied with the likeness of my darling little boys, Willie & Taddie, taken in 1861- they will answer very well for the picture you propose painting. Even in that likeness of Willie justice is not done him; he was a very beautiful boy with a most spiritual expression of face. He was a most peculiarly religious child with great amiability and cheerfulness of character- it is impossible for time to alleviate the anguish of such irreparable losses- only the grace of God can calm our grief & still the tempest. I wish you could have known that dear boy, for child he scarcely seemed to me. So unlike Taddie, yet so devoted to him- their love for each other was charming to behold."

*Underlining is Mary Lincoln's

Elizabeth (Todd) Grimsley - "Willie was a noble, beautiful boy of eleven years, of great mental activity, unusual intelligence, wonderful memory, methodical, frank and loving, a counterpart of his father, save that he [Willie] was handsome. The angel of death had borne away the idolized boy, and with it had gone part of the doting mother's heart also, which was never more to find peace."

Emilie (Todd) Helm - "Willie was a beautiful boy, intelligent, polite, observant, careful of the comfort of others and courtly in his manners."

Julia (Taft) Bayne - "Willie was the most lovable boy I ever knew, bright, sensible, sweet-tempered and gentle-mannered. One day he gave me a photograph of himself and a *little golden [dog] charm and told me he loved me. Of course, I was interested in boys my own age, but I will treasure that little charm always."

*Efforts to track down descendants of Julia who may have kept Willie's charm were unsuccessful.

Benjamin Brown French (September 4, 1800 - April 12, 1870), Lincoln family friend - "Mrs. Lincoln did all a mother ought or could do during Willie's sickness- she never left his side after he became dangerously ill & almost wore herself out with watching, and she mourns as no one but a mother can at her son's death."

Dr. Robert King Stone, Lincoln family physician in Washington - "In addition to traditional medicines, I tried all the folk medicines in Washington, from Peruvian bark to beef tea to treat this new ague, but I could not save him."

Former President Franklin Pierce (November 23, 1804 - October 8, 1869) - "The impulse to write you [Lincoln] the moment I heard of your great domestic affliction was very strong, but it brought back the crushing sorrow which befell me just before I went to Washington in 1853 [Pierce's young son Benjamin "Bennie" Pierce April 13, 1841 - January 6, 1853, was killed in a train accident] with such power that I felt your grief, to be too sacred for intrusion. Even in this hour, so full of danger to our country, and of trial and anxiety to all good men your thoughts, will be, of your cherished boy, who will nestle in your heart, until you meet him in the new life, when tears and toil and conflict will be unknown. I realize how vain it would be, to suggest sources of consolation. There can be but one refuge in such an hour, but one remedy for smitten hearts, which, which is to trust in Him 'who doeth all things well', and leave the rest to the, 'time comforter and only healer when he heart hath broke'. With Mrs. Pierce's and my best wishes, and truest sympathy for Mrs. Lincoln and yourself, I am very truly, Yr. friend."

General George McClellan - "I have not felt authorized to intrude upon you personally in the midst of the deep distress I know you feel in the sad calamity that had befallen you and your family. Yet I cannot refrain from expressing to you the sincere and deep sympathy I feel for you. You have been kind and true friend in the midst of the great cares and difficulties by which we have been surrounded during the past few months. Your confidence has upheld me when I otherwise should have felt weak. I wish to not only assure you and your family that I have felt the deepest sympathy in your affliction."

William Florville, December 27, 1863 ("Billy" the Barber, Lincoln's dear friend and barber in Springfield) - "I was surprised at the announcement at the death of your son Willy. I thought him a smart boy for his age, so considerate, so manly, his knowledge and good sense far exceeding most boys more advanced in years, Yet the time comes to us all, all must die."

"My family are all well. My son William is married and in business for himself. I am occupying the same place in which I was when you left. Tell Taddie that his [and Willie's] dog [Fido] is alive and kicking, doing well. He stays mostly at John E. Roll's with his Boys who are about the age now that Tad & Willy were when they left for Washington."

"Your residence here is kept in good order. Mr. Tilton (Lucian Tilton July 10, 1812 - March 19, 1877 President of the Great Western Railroad) has no children to ruin things. Mrs. Tilton and Miss Tilton are very strong Union ladies who do a great deal for the Soldiers who are suffering so much for us & to sustain the Government."

"Please accept my best wishes for yourself and family."

Horatio Nelson Taft, Sr. from his diary, Thursday, February 20, 1862 - "We hear tonight with much sorrow that our little friend Willie Lincoln died at 5 p. m. He had been sick for near three weeks with Typhoid fever [probably small pox as well]. Bud had been to see him or inquire about him almost every day. He and his mother were there yesterday about noon. Willie was then thought to be better [dying people often have a brief resurgence of lucidity and apparent recovery shortly before the end]. He was an amiable, good-hearted boy; was here with our boys almost every day or our boys were there [the White House]. We all got much attached to him and Tad his brother. He had more judgment and foresight than any boy his age that I have ever known; poor Willie we all lament."

Alexander Williamson in the *New York World,* March 8, 1862 - "William Wallace Lincoln, who died last week, was a remarkably bright boy for one of his years, and his tutor is fond of telling stories of his aptitude in mastering the studies which he was pursuing. His memory was so wonderfully retentive that he had only to go over once or twice a page of his speller and definer, and the impression so fixed that he went through without hesitation of blundering, and his other studies in proportion. Little Willie was a constant attendant at the Sabbath-school, and always manifested a deep interest in the instruction of counsel there imparted to him. He confided in me that he wanted to become either a preacher or teacher."

Elizabeth Keckly from her memoir *Behind the Scenes* (1866) - "Willie was so delighted with his little pony, that he insisted on riding it every day. The weather was changeable, and exposure resulted in a severe cold which deepened into fever. He was very sick and I was summoned to his bedside. It was sad to see the poor boy suffer. Always of a delicate constitution, he could not resist the strong inroads of disease. The days dragged wearily by, and he grew weaker and more shadowlike. The light faded from his eyes and the death dew gathered on his brow. He was his mother's favorite and she doted on him. It grieved her sorely to see him suffer. When able to be about he was almost constantly by her side. When I would go into her room, almost always I found blue-eyed Willie there, reading from an open book, or curled up in a chair with pencil and paper in hand. He had a decidedly literary taste, and was a studious boy. He lingered a few more [days] and died. God called the beautiful spirit home."

Thomas H. Nelson (August 12, 1824 - March 14, 1896), Lincoln friend - "The last steamer brought the sad tidings of the death of your son Willie. Without intending to intrude upon your private sorrows, I must be permitted to express my cordial sympathy with Mrs. Lincoln and yourself in this painful bereavement. I knew the little boy well. His rare qualities of head and heart won for him the love and admiration of all who knew him, and gave promise of future excellence, while his fine physical organization seem to indicate long life and vigorous health."

"Mrs. Nelson and myself, from whom our bright little boy [Thomas H. Nelson 1854- April 1860] of nearly the same age with Willie, was suddenly taken, know how deep must be your sorrow and how keen your anguish, in sustaining a loss so grievous and irreparable. But 'the Lord gave and the Lord hath taken away, blessed be the name of the Lord'."

"God grant to you, sir, health and strength, to enable you to discharge the duties of your great office, in this, the most eventful and trying epoch of our Country's history, that you may add luster to your name and promote the safety, glory and happiness of our beloved Union."

Nathaniel Parker Willis, from the *Home Journal* March 1862 - [Elizabeth (Todd) Grimsley said in her memoir *Six Months In the White House*, that he {Willis} had an "inordinate vanity" and "he was a man ready to take advantage of a any familiar footing afforded him. This, however, we could forgive because of his <u>excessive</u> fondness for Willie."] *Underling is Grimsley's

"This little fellow had his acquaintances among his father's friends, and I chance to be one of them. He never failed to seek me out in a crowd, shake hands, and make some pleasant remark; and this; in a boy of eleven years of age, was, to say the least, endearing to a stranger. But he had more than mere affectionateness. His self possession- aplomb, as the French call it- was extraordinary. I was one day passing the White House, when he was outside with a play-fellow on the sidewalk. Mr. Seward drove in with Prince Napoleon and two of his suite in their carriage, and, in a mock-heroic way- terms of intimacy existing between the boy and the Secretary, the official gentleman took off his hat, and the Napoleon did the same, all making the young prince President a ceremonious salute. Not a bit staggered with the homage, Willie drew himself up to his full height, took off his little hat with graceful self-possession, and bowed down formally to the ground, like a little ambassador. They drove past and he went on unconcernedly with his play: the impromptu readiness and good judgment being clearly a part of his nature. His genial and open expression of countenance was none the less ingenuous and fearless for a certain tincture of fun; and it was in the mingling of qualities that he so faithfully resembles his father."

"With all the splendor that was around this little fellow in his new home he was bravely and beautifully himself and that only. A wild-flower transplanted from the prairie to the hothouse, he retained his prairie habits, unalterably pure and simple, till he died. His leading trait seemed to a fearless and kindly frankness, willing that everything should be as different as it pleased, but resting unmoved in his own conscious singleheartedness. I found I was studying him irresistibly, as one of the sweet problems of childhood that the world is blessed with in rare places, and the news of his death (I was absent from Washington on a visit to my own children at the time) came to me like a knell heard un- expectedly at a merry-making."

"On the day of the funeral I went before the hour, to take a farewell look at the dear boy; for they had embalmed him to send him home to the West- to sleep under the sod of his own valley- and the coffin-lid was to be closed before the service. The family had just taken their leave of him, and the servants and nurses were seeing him for the last time- and with tears and sobs wholly unrestrained, for he was loved liked an idol by every one of them. He lay with eyes closed- his brown hair parted as we had known it- pale in the slumber of death; but otherwise unchanged, for he was dressed as if for the evening, and held in one of his hands, crossed upon is breast, a bunch of exquisite flowers- a message coming from his mother, while we were looking upon him, that those flowers might be preserved for her. She was lying sick in her bed, worn out with grief and overwatching."

"The funeral was very touching. Of the entertainments in the East Room the boy had been- for those now assembled more especially- a most life-giving variation. With bright face, and his apt greetings and replies, he was remembered in every part of the crimson-curtained hall built only for pleasure- of all the crowds, each night, certainly he was the one least likely to be Death's first mark. He was his father's favorite. They were intimates- often seen hand in hand. And there sat the man, with a burden on his brain- staggering from a blow like a taking from of his child! His men of power sat around him- McClellan with a moist eye when bowed to the prayer, as I could see from where I stood; and Chase and Seward with their austere features at work; and senators and ambassadors, and soldiers, all struggling with their tears- great hearts sorrowing with the President as a stricken man and a brother. That God may give him strength for all his burdens is, I am sure, at present the prayer of a nation."

*Underlining is Willis's.

Emily J. Bugbee (December 19, 1837 - July 8, 1913) from *The Little Corporal*, July 1865 - "Willie Lincoln, a name that will forever be sweetly linked with the undying memory of our martyred President. For, together they went, out in life, from their quiet home in Illinois to the lofty halls of the presidential mansion, and, together they came back with silent lips and folded hand, sleeping peacefully in death; the mission of each accomplished, the work of life all done. The little boy, and the great statesman! There is something beautiful in the thought of the sweet mission Willie's death may have accomplished; how far-reaching its influence, who shall tell. His life of joy and gladness faded out in troublesome times, and the shadow of a great sorrow was added to that heart already burdened with the weight of a periled nation's care. It seems to me that, as his spirit went upward, the door of heaven was left ajar to the spiritual eye of Abraham Lincoln, and, then often, amid his weariness and toil, he caught glimpses of the glory to be revealed, and above the joy, jar and tumult of earth's discordant passions, came often- to soothe his troubled spirit- a sound of heavenly harmony in which was mingled the voice of his departed child and that noble heart, always tender and generous, grew more and more softened and subdued, under this silent, unseen influence, and he wrought, and wept, and prayed unceasingly, for the great good of the nation, and the world; his warm sympathies gushing out even to his enemies."

"Willie, though absent, was ever present with his Father, for he said on one occasion to an officer of the Army, 'Do you ever find yourself talking with the dead? Since Willie died I find myself talking to him as if he were with me.' Ah! Who knows what precious communing were those? Who knows how silently and sweetly the Angel Boy was leading the Father onward, and showing him the mysteries of the Kingdom? And who knows what sure foreshadowings thrilled that great yearning heart, of the not distant time, when, on the other shore, he should clasp again the hand of his boy, and together they should stray by the still waters, and in the green pastures of the better land?"

"But three years were they divided; to Willie, wandering amid the glories of Heaven, they were but so many golden hours; to his Father, such years as no man ever lived before, in which the heart-throbs of a lifetime were condensed, and a sublime mission was accomplished."

"And then another shadow fell upon the presidential mansion, in comparison to which, the shadow Willie's coffin had cast, was oh so small. That fell directly on the hearts of parents and brothers, but this fell dark and black over a great nation, aye, over the world. But they took up the sleeping boy tenderly, and laid him by the mighty dead, and brought them onward, while cannons boomed, and bells tolled, and tears fell like autumn rain, and pure white flowers were strewn over all the long funeral way, till at last they rest side by side near the dear home they left four years ago, in life, and happiness, and health. Loving in their lives and in their deaths not divided."

*Underlining is Bugbee's.

Dr. Phineas D. Gurley, Pastor, New York Avenue Presbyterian Church, funeral oration and elegy, Monday, February 24, 1862, 2 p.m. - "Sad and solemn is the occasion that brings us here today. A dark shadow of affliction has suddenly fallen upon this habitation, and on the hearts of its inmates. The news thereof has already gone forth to the extremities of the country."

"The Nation has heard it with deep and tender emotions. The eye of the Nation is moistened with tears, as it turns today to the Presidential Mansion; the heart of the Nation sympathizes with its Chief Magistrate, while to the unprecedented weight of civil care which presses on him is added the burden of his great domestic sorrow, and the prayer of the Nation ascends to Heaven on his behalf, and on the behalf of his weeping family, that God's grace may be sufficient for them, and that in this hour of sore bereavement and trial, they may have the presence and succor of Him, who has said, 'Come unto me all you that labor and our heavy laden, and I will give you rest.'"

"Oh that they may be able to lay their head upon His infinite bosom, and find, as many other smitten ones have found, that He is their truest refuge and strength; a very present help in trouble."

'The beloved youth, whose death we now here lament, was a child of great high intelligence and peculiar promise. He possessed many excellent qualities of mind and heart, which greatly endeared him, not only to the family circle of which he was a member, but to his youthful companions, and to all his acquaintances and friends."

"His mind was active, inquisitive and conscientious; his disposition amiable and affectionate; his impulses were kind and generous, and his words and manner were gentle and attractive. It is easy to see how a child, thus endowed, would, in the course of eleven years, entwine himself around the hearts of those who knew him best; nor can we wonder that the grief of his affectionate mother today is like that of Rachel weeping for her children and refusing to be comforted because they were not."

"His sickness was an attack of fever, threatening from the beginning, and painfully productive mental wandering and delirium. All that the tenderest parental care and watching, and the most assiduous and skillful medical treatment could do, was done; and though at times, even in the latest stages of the disease, his symptoms were regarded as favorable, and inspired a faint and wavering hope that he was not beyond recovery. Still the insidious malady, day after day, pursued its course unchecked, and on Thursday last, at the hour of five in the afternoon, the silver cord was loosed. The golden bowl was broken, and the emancipated spirit returned to God, who gave it."

"That departure was a sore bereavement to the parents and brothers; but while they weep, they also rejoice in the confidence that their loss is the unspeakable and eternal gain of the departed; for they believe as well as they may, that he has gone to Him who said, 'Suffer the little children to come onto me, and forbid them not, for of such is the Kingdom of Heaven;' and that now, with kindred spirits, and with a departed brother, [Eddy] who he never saw on earth, he beholds the glory and sings the praises of the Redeemer. Blessed be God."

> "There is a world above
> Where sorrow is unknown;
> A long eternity of love,
> Formed for the good alone;
> And faith beholds the dying here
> Translated to the glorious sphere."

"It is well for us, and very comforting, on such an occasion as this, to get a clear and scriptural view of the providence of God. His kingdom ruleth over all. All those events which in anyways affect our condition and happiness are in His hands and at his disposal. Disease and death are his messengers; they go forth at his bidding, and their fearful worth is limited or extended according to the good pleasure of his will."

"Not a sparrow falls to the ground without his direction; much less anyone of the human family, for we are of more value than many sparrows."

"We may be sure, - therefore, bereaved parents and all the children of sorrow may be sure, - that their affliction has not come forth out of the dust, nor be their trouble sprung out of the ground."

"It is well-ordered procedure of their Father and their God. A mysterious dealing that many consider it, but still it is his dealing, and while they mourn He is saying to them, as the Lord Jesus once said to his Disciples when they were perplexed by his conduct. 'What we need in the hour of trial, and what we should seek by earnest prayer, is confidence in Him who sees the end from the beginning and doeth all things well."

"Only let us bow in His presence with a humble and teachable spirit; only let us be still and know that He is God.; only let us acknowledge His hand, and hear His voice, and inquire after His will, and seek His Holy Spirit as our counselor and guide, in all, in the end, will be well. In His light, by His grace our sorrows will be sanctified-they will be made a blessing to our souls- and by and by we shall have occasion to say, with blended gratitude and rejoicing, 'It is good for us to know that we have been afflicted!'"

> "Heaven but tries our virtues by affliction;
> And oft the cloud that wraps the present hour
> Serves to brighten all our future days."

Extracts from an unpublished manuscript (ca: 1866) by Dr. Phineas D. Gurley from the book *Latest Light on Abraham Lincoln* (1917) by Ervin Sylvester Chapman (June 1838 - August 30, 1921), - "On account of the nature of [Willie's] disease a varioloid, [now known as a variola is a normally non-fatal smallpox strain often caused by a slight reaction to being vaccinated] his funeral was as private as possible [since the word s varioloid and smallpox created panic]. I was with the President often during these dark hours. Willie's death was a great blow to Mr. Lincoln, coming as it did in the midst of the war, when his burdens seemed already greater than he could bear. The little boy was always interested in the war and used to go down to the White House stables and read the battle news to the employees and talk over the outcome. These men all loved him, and thought for one of his years, he was most unusual. When he was dying he said to me, 'Doctor Gurley, I have six one dollar gold pieces [actually five according to Mrs. Lincoln who gave them to Dr. Gurley after Willie's passing] in my bank over there on the mantel. Please send them to the missionaries for me.' After his death those six one dollar pieces were shown to my Sunday School and the scholars were informed of Willie's request."

ODE FOR WILLIE

There never was a more
    beloved boy;
A blooming bud of innocence
    and joy;
Plucked by smallpox and typhoid
    at eleven;
Now a white dove of Peace
    in Heaven;
Meek and mild, a special
    gifted boy;
Empathic and compassionate
    far beyond his years,
Now for Abe and Mary a void
    filled only with tears.

The black mourning crepe
    ripples in the wicked wind;
Two white horses
    strain against the gusts;
In Oak Hill Cemetery
    in the Carroll Vault
All is still and silent;
    In the White House
Pain fills every cold corner.

Donald Motier - February 20, 2012

Afterword

IN HIS SHORT life Willie Lincoln touched the hearts, minds and souls of many people of all ages and backgrounds. Whether it were members of his father's staff, Cabinet, members of Congress, governors, generals, journalists, poets, pastors, teachers, servants, the common soldier or even foreign princes and his friends and playmates from Springfield, such as the devoted Henry Remann who saved Willie's letters, Edward "Eddie" Rathburn, Jr. and Horatio "Bud" Nelson Taft, Jr., his 15-year-old best friend in Washington who sat vigil at Willie's bedside holding his hand to the end and last but not least the white and Black street urchins and Black children of the White House servants he befriended. He was loved by them all and dearly missed.

Willie was the son most like his father in temperament and intelligence, indeed, an exact counterpart or clone of Abe. He had the same qualities of honesty, frankness, loving-kindness, generosity, empathy, compassion and spirituality as his father. He loved to write poetry, little sermons and speeches, keep accurate railroad timetables, newspaper articles about battles and elections and was a faithful attendee of Sunday School and classes of Alexander Williamson. He imitated his father in mannerism, carrying his head slightly to one side as his father did. Willie possessed, rare among boys his age, a natural instinct for justice and empathy. Even on the day he died he was thinking of others.

He asked both his mother and his pastor Dr. Phineas Gurley to take his savings, six one dollar coins and give them to the Sunday School Mission Program.

Although he was an active outdoor boy, his immune system may have been weakened by tubercular symptoms and especially by a month-long bout with scarlet fever in June and July of 1860 that may have resulted in heart valve damage and a bad case of measles in March 1861 did not help matters. The changeable weather of Washington, dust, offal and garbage-filled canal and swamp nearby, influx of thousands of troops into the city in 1861 with many encamped next to the Potomac River with open latrine ditches emptying directly into the water made it dangerous for the health of anyone but especially for a little boy from a small town in the Midwest with an already compromised immune system. In December 1861 through February 1862 typhoid fever and small pox were epidemic among the troops and populace. As a precaution, the Taft children were vaccinated and re-vaccinated against small pox and so were Willie and Tad. On Saturday, January 25, 1862 Willie received a pony as a gift. He loved that pony and rode it around the White House grounds regardless of the changeable weather and his mother's admonitions. One day the weather was balmy and in the 60s and the next would have light snow, sleet, freezing rain, or rain. On February 5th Willie came down with what appeared to be a bad cold with a high fever. His mother initially kept him wrapped in blankets by the fireplace but when his fever worsened, he was put to bed in the Prince of Wales Room so named for the prince who had stayed there during the Buchanan administration. Dr. Robert King Stone, the Lincoln family physician in Washington, was called and at first he described Willie's illness as "bilious fever" then later "fever with a typhoid character" and finally a "new ague" meaning he didn't really know what disease or diseases Willie suffered from.

Potable water for drinking was pumped into the lower levels of the White House beginning in 1833 from a well in Franklin Square. There were two, possibly three hydrants; one in the basement corridor, one in the main floor butler's pantry where the dishes were washed in a marble sink, and perhaps one in the kitchen. However, water for drinking from Great Falls did not arrive at the White House by aqueduct till December 5, 1863 and presumably brought drinking water to the second floor living quarters. Cold Potomac River water for washing only ordered by Buchanan was installed in all the second floor family quarters in the spring of 1861. Marble-topped wash stands with fancy painted porcelain sinks were installed in all the second floor rooms except the library. Each had a single hydrant.

If indeed Willie contracted typhoid, knowing boys if their pitcher on the wash stand was empty on a cold evening in January 1862 perhaps around the same time Willie received his pony, (since the incubation for typhoid is 10-14 days) he and Tad waking up thirsty and not feeling like running down the drafty hall and downstairs in their red nightshirts and bare feet, thinking a little wouldn't hurt, took drinks from the Potomac River water hydrant in their room thus contracting typhoid. It is interesting to note that the record indicates *no one else, not the Taft boys, White House staff or the president and Mrs. Lincoln were sick with typhoid symptoms at that time.* This would point to a single source for the boys' disease. Assuming that Willie, whose immune system was already weak, came into the drafty, smelly White House on that day February 5, 1862 soaked and muddy from riding his pony in the cold rain, sleet or snow, had picked-up a cold virus from someone the day before but stubbornly insisted on riding his pony and contracted typhoid (and Tad also) from drinking the Potomac Water around January 22-26, then developed on top of those infections a varioloid (variola), a usually nonfatal small pox strain from being re-vaccinated. In most people this would have only resulted in a mild reaction, but with Willie's weakened and vulnerable condition and having a bad cold that probably developed into bronchial pneumonia and contracting typhoid, it was catch-22 fatal. The combined symptoms of severe headache, fever, loss of appetite, malaise, abdominal pain, constipation, diarrhea, with small pink spots appearing on his abdomen, then finally delirium, intestinal hemorrhaging in the case of the typhoid resulting in sepsis, a cough, difficulty breathing, wheezing in the case of bronchial pneumonia, appearance of some pustules, rash and kidney damage from the small pox racked the poor little body. All the doctors' traditional and home remedies of the time did nothing to alleviate his suffering. Laudanum given in small doses as it restricts breathing as he was constantly gasping for breath may have briefly eased his unimaginable suffering.

After careful research although it will never be known for sure, I believe as does Lincoln scholar Dr. Wayne Temple that Willie died of *multiple* causes and diseases. Today, if caught early, antibiotics such as penicillin, ampicillin and chloramphenicol would have cured him in a week.

There is no doubt that Willie's death nearly drove Mary Lincoln into the depths of madness and Lincoln warned her if she didn't get hold of herself she would "end up on the building (asylum) on the hill." She compensated by relying on dream "contacts" with Willie, Eddie and her half-brother Confederate soldier Alexander Todd killed in the Battle of Baton Rouge and charlatan mediums that fed her survival guilt for not forcing Willie to stay indoors instead of riding his pony in bad weather; not that in the end it would have made any difference if typhoid and small pox had been incubating in him for 10-14 days. Willie's death had also awakened her sense of early abandonment that had begun in childhood with the death of her mother when Mary was seven and had continued with little Eddy's death of tuberculosis on February 1, 1850. The deaths of two of her half-brothers during the Civil War, Lincoln's assassination, and the death of Tad at 18 on July 16, 1871 took its final toll and it seems she almost willed herself to die eleven years later almost on the anniversary of Tad's death on July 17, 1882. Robert Lincoln also died in July on the 25th in 1926.

The effect on Tad of Willie's death cannot be minimized . He could no longer play with his brother's toys, especially Willie's train cars that his mother had sent to her nephew in Springfield, Edward Lewis Baker, Jr. Even two years after Willie's death when Julia Taft visited the White house [the Taft boys and Julia had not been to the White House since Willie died except briefly by Bud at the viewing. Mrs. Lincoln forbade them because "they remind me too much of my loss"] upon seeing Julia Tad threw himself on the floor in throes of tears and screams. Although understandable to a point, Mary Lincoln's refusal to allow the Taft boys to come back left Tad alone without close playmates and alone with his grief. Tad didn't leave a written record of his short life. Maybe it was just too painful to write about even when he was older and did well in schools in Europe. Dr. Phineas Gurley was the person to tell Tad about his father's death on the morning of April 15, 1865. "Taddy, your Pa is dead!" Poor Tad shocked to his little boy core replied, "O what shall I do? What SHALL I do? My Brother is dead! My Father is dead! O what shall I do?"

The deaths of his mother, sister and infant brother in childhood sowed the seeds of Lincoln's melancholy and depression later in life. The losses of Anne Rutledge (January 7, 1813 - August 25, 1835), his first love and son Eddy in 1850 added to his fatalistic and somber attitude abut life and mortality. The shock of the deaths of his close family friends Colonel Elmer Ellsworth in May 1961 and Colonel Edward Baker in October 1861 and the rising death toll in the war took a terrible toll on his emotional health. The most devastating blow he suffered in the White House was the horrible suffering and death of Willie on February 20, 1862. After Willie's entombment in the Carroll Vault in Oak Hill Cemetery in Georgetown, Lincoln purportedly returned at least two times in the week following Willie's death to have the caretaker unlock the vault and have Willie's coffin slid out of the crypt and out of the narrow tiled vault floor and opened outside in the cold February night so he could gaze once more on his beloved boy's countenance and "talk" to him. He could not let go. He had "dream conversations" with Willie as if he was with him only to wake up in the morning realizing it was *only a dream*. Unlike

Mary Lincoln and Tad, Abe wanted reminders of Willie around him and kept some of Willie's small toys on his office desk and a painting Willie had done of Illinois on the mantel above the fireplace. During a visit by close friend Orville Browning in June 1862 after church, Lincoln took him into the library and showed him a box of "memoranda" he had just found that Willie had kept in the Library that included railroad tables, clippings of newspaper articles about battles, the inaugurations of his father and the governor of Illinois, poems and little speeches. Although Lincoln was never officially a member of any church, he often quoted the Bible in his speeches and conversations and was a spiritual person. After Willie's death he had long sorrowful conversations about mortality and Heaven with various clergy who assured him that "Willie lives!" In May 1862 while on a trip to Fort Monroe during a tearful conversation with an officer named LeGrand Cannon Lincoln quoted Shakespeare from *King John* 3:3, lines that also gave him hope:

"And, Father Cardinal, I have heard you say
That we shall see and know our friends in Heaven;
If that be true, I shall see my boy again."

I wish I could have known Willie, but in a way I *have*, for while researching my family tree I found that Willie is my *3rd cousin two times removed! [see addenda]. While writing the manuscript I often had the unsettling but not unpleasant impression that Willie was looking over my shoulder as I wrote [there is an 11" x 14" photo of Willie with his Uncle s' walking stick in a antique oval frame on the wall behind me and his eyes seemed to be looking at and through me]. Also, during the years of writing there were the incredibly vivid dreams [genetic memory?] of being right there in the White House and on the grounds in 1861-62 viewing details not found in books. In fact, I've often felt that *Willie wrote the two previous historical novels and this biography…I was just the vehicle!*

*According to both the 2008 CD Version of Lite Family Tree Maker by Ancestry.com and the current online 2018 Ancestry.com Willie IS my 3rd cousin two times removed.

It has been a labor of love. God Bless You Willie. Love Is Eternal.

WILLIE LINCOLN'S BEST FRIENDS

WILLIE'S BEST FRIENDS in life were Henry Christian Remann, Jr. (April 6, 1850 - February 26, 1920), and Edward "Eddie" Rathbun, Jr. (1848 - 1862) in Springfield and Horatio "Bud" Nelson Taft, Jr. (January 15, 1847 - January 6, 1915) in Washington.

Henry Christian Remann, Jr. was born in Springfield at 802 S. 8th Street the son of Henry Christian Remann, Sr. (? - December 10, 1849) and Mary (Black) Remann (March 5, 1823 - February 7, 1888), who came to Springfield from Vandalia, Illinois a short time before their son Henry Jr. was born. Henry Sr. was a native of Saxony, Germany and his mother was of old Puritan stock from Lee, Massachusetts.

Henry was the same age as Willie and lived on the same block at the end of 8th Street. Willie and Henry were constant playmates, both avid readers and of a more refined nature than most boys their age but not above childish pranks.

One afternoon Henry went to the Lincoln home and was met at the door by Abe who told him all the boys were away. Sensing disappointment, Abe asked if he could do anything for him. Henry said that Robert had promised to lend him a book to read. "Well," Said Abe, "A boy should have a book to read when he wants one; come with me." Together they went up to Robert's room and selected *Don Quixote* and

Henry went away happy. Henry corresponded with Willie in 1861 and possibly into 1862 but only four letters survive that Willie wrote to Henry; May 3, May 25 and September 30, 1861 from Washington that Henry saved. And an earlier letter from the Tremont Hotel in Chicago where Abe and Willie were staying dated June 6, 1859 to Henry from Willie.

Henry graduated from Springfield High School in 1866 as did Edward J. McClernand, another friend of Willie's and in Willie's May 25, 1861 letter to Henry, Willie expressed his condolences at the death of Edward's mother. Had Willie lived and not moved to Washington he would have graduated with Henry and Edward from Springfield High. In the 1910 Springfield High School yearbook *Capitoline* in the Alumni Section, Henry is listed as living at 402 S. 8th Street and Edward in Omaha, Nebraska.

After Henry graduated from high school, he was taken into the office of his uncle, George Nelson Black (March 15, 1833 - April 22, 1908), who at that time was the junior member of the firm of John Williams (September 11, 1808 - May 29, 1890) and Company, proprietors of the general store on the north side of the square, The establishment was located in the building occupied [1920] by Scotch Woolen Mills Company. Henry remained with Mr. Black in various capacities and in numerous enterprises up until the time of the latter's retirement from business on account of ill health in 1905. At that time Henry was appointed City Librarian, a post he held continuously until his death. In addition to holding this office Henry served as City Comptroller under Mayor James Maurice Garland (September 26, 1835 - June 29, 1931).

During his tenure as City Librarian at the Lincoln Library, the library experienced an enormous growth and through various means introduced by Henry the public learned to patronize the institution to a greater extent than ever before in its history. Sub-stations [branch libraries] were established throughout the city. The library was up-to-date and thousands were accustomed to visiting it every week. Henry had become a familiar figure in Springfield and was exceedingly well-known throughout the city.

Henry was a man of retiring disposition and possessed deep literary and musical tastes. He had traveled extensively in this country and abroad. He was well informed and spoke intelligently on practically every subject of general interest.

Henry never married and remained a lifelong bachelor living at 629 South Walnut Street with his sister Mary.

Henry evidently contracted influenza [Spanish?] around the 20th of February 1920 and died at 2:45 in the afternoon of February 26 at his home of lobar pneumonia and heart failure [death certificate] according to the attending physician Dr. George F. Sleurbeer [sp.?]. He was 69. Like his long lost beloved boyhood friend Willie, Henry died in February. The funeral was held Saturday, February 28, 1920 at 2:30 in the afternoon at his church the First Presbyterian, the same church the Lincolns had attended and rented a pew after the death of Eddy Lincoln in 1850. The Reverend John D. Thomas D.D. (1877 - 1962) officiated. A quartet sang "Crossing The Bar" and several other selections. Henry was interred next to the rest of is family in Oak Ridge Cemetery, Block 7, Lot 117 not far from the Lincoln Tomb. As in life, Henry and Willie were neighbors again.

Edward "Eddie" Rathbun, Jr., aka Edwin Rathbun, Edwin Rathbone was born in Brooklyn, New York in 1848, the son of Edward Rathbun, Sr. (September 17, 1823 - May 15, 1854) and Hannah Stanton Miner (1828 - October 28, 1878). They were married on April 11, 1846 in Brooklyn. Edward Rathbun was born in Connecticut. Hannah was also born in Connecticut.

The 1855 Special New York Census lists Eddie as living in Brooklyn, Ward 10, Kings Co. NY, District E.D.1, House #38, Line 13, age 5. Hannah moved to Springfield, Illinois in 1856 after the death of her husband with her two sons Edward, Jr. and James Miner Rathbun (1853 - August 5, 1898) to live with her brother and sister-in-law the

Reverend and Mrs. Noyes W. Miner. The Miners were renting the Lushbaugh home directly across from the Lincolns on what is now known as the Burch Lot at 8th and Jackson Sts. At this time Rev. Miner was the pastor of the First Baptist Church at 7th and Adam Sts. Not long after Hannah's arrival both boys had mishaps requiring medical attention. Dr. John Henry Shearer (1827 - December 14, 1898) arrived at the home to attend to them. His help led to a friendship that eventually led to marriage with Hannah on June 12, 1858. The Miners moved to other quarters leaving the couple as Lincoln neighbors 1858-59. Hannah became close friends with Mary Lincoln as sons Eddie and James did with Willie and Tad, respectively. The family moved to Wellsboro, Tioga County, Pennsylvania in 1859 hoping the change in climate might help Dr. Shearer's chronic tubercular condition. The 1860 Pennsylvania Census lists Edward Rathbun age 12 living in Wellsboro. Hannah continued to correspond with Mary Lincoln and Hannah and the boys accompanied Mary, Willie and Tad on vacation to Long Branch, New Jersey in August 1861. Hannah was at that time pregnant and told Willie that if it was a boy she would name it after him. Willie said he was quite proud that someone would want to. On October 28, 1861 Hannah gave birth to a son whom was promptly christened William Lincoln Shearer.

Sadly, sometime in 1862 Edward "Eddie" Rathbun, Jr. died in Wellsboro at age 14 possibly of tuberculosis contracted from his stepfather. Eddie is buried next to his father Edward Rathbun, Sr. in Wood Lawn Cemetery in Wellsville, Allegany County, New York as is his brother James (James Miner Rathbun 1852/3 - August 5, 1898), his sister-in-law Ida (White) Rathbun 1856 - March 21, 1938), and niece Hannah Adele Rathbun (October 3, 1880 - June 26, 1979), all listed on a flat stone marker. The cemetery burial record there lists the date 1862 for the death of Eddie and this is probably correct as it came from a longtime caretaker. Mary Lincoln, in a letter to Hannah (Rathbun) Shearer dated November 1864 lamenting Willie's death, refers to Eddie's death,"… doubtless our angel boys are reunited [in

Heaven] as *they loved each other so much* on earth." This could imply Eddie died sometime earlier that month or it may be that Mary, as she did frequently for years after Willie's death, was just re-lamenting both boys passing. A thorough search on Ancestry.com, Newspapers.com and regional sources did not turn up a date for poor Eddie's demise. Mary Lincoln continued to correspond with Hannah Rathbun Shearer until her (Hannah's) death on October 20, 1878.

William Lincoln Shearer (October 21, 1861 - February 10, 1932) became a well known Pennsylvania journalist and Willie would have been very proud of him.

Horatio Nelson Taft, Jr. nicknamed "Bud" was born January 15, 1847 in Lyons, New York the son of Horatio Nelson Taft, Sr. (January 13, 1806 - April 15, 1888) and Mary (Cook) Taft (July 10, 1812 - April 5, 1905). Mr. Taft was born in Savoy, Massachusetts and settled in Lyons in 1822. Mrs. Taft was from Bridge-Hampton, New York. The couple were married in 1843.

Bud was baptized (as was his author [*Tad Lincoln's Father*] sister Julia (Taft) Bayne (March 8, 1845 - December 14, 1933) in the Lyons Grace Episcopal Church. Bud entered First Grade at the Lyons Union School in the year ending March 1854. Julia was in the Second Grade the same year. The senior Taft was instrumental in founding the Lyons Union School. Bud attended the school through the Sixth Grade.

In 1856 Horatio Nelson Taft, Sr. was appointed Chief Examiner in the United States Patent Office by President James Buchanan. Bud and the rest of the family joined him in Washington in 1859 where they resided first on I Street then on L Street near Franklin Square. In early March of 1861 shortly after President Lincoln's inauguration Mrs. Lincoln, concerned that Willie and Tad had no friends to play with in Washington [and perhaps worried they'd take up with the Washington street urchins] arranged a meeting with the Taft children; Julia 16, Bud, 14, Holly [Halsey Cook Taft] 11, and Willie [William Cook Taft] 7, in the Conservatory of the White House. The children's father was a friend of Abraham Lincoln's. Bud and Willie Lincoln and Holly and Tad became fast friends and from that day onward through 1861 and up until Willie Lincoln's tragic death February 20, 1862 they were inseparable. The Lincoln boys were either at the Taft's or the Taft boys were at the White House on a daily basis often staying overnight. Although Bud was four years older than Willie [age 10 in 1861], Willie, who was intellectually advanced and emotionally mature for his age, the difference was inconsequential and they were devoted to each other. Both were more reserved that their younger brothers, loved to read and Bud had an artistic bent drawing and sculpting soldiers, houses, ships and animals quite well and Willie had a literary bent writing credible poems, letters and little speeches (imitation of his father) and sermons.

The increasing threat of an invasion of Washington by the rebels made Mr. Taft fear for the safety of his family and late in September 1861 he gave up the house on L Street he had been renting and sold most of their furniture. Only through the intervention of Mrs. Lincoln who didn't want her boys to lose their playmates, was Mr. Taft's fears allayed and he was persuaded to stay. On October 1st, 1861 the family moved to 346 9th Street West.

In July of 1861, Bud, with the recommendation of President Lincoln had applied for the position of Page in the House of Representatives but by December was still waiting for an answer. It is not known whether he ever received a reply but it appears Bud didn't get the position as he continued uninterrupted as Willie's best friend and daily playmate until Willie's death. After Willie's death, Mary Lincoln refused to allow the Taft boys to come to the White House to play with Tad as they were too much of a reminder of Willie although this left poor Tad basically alone with no one to play with except the street urchins. Bud was obviously in despair after Willie's death as he loved him very much being at his bedside holding Willie's hand virtuously nonstop for the last few days of Willie's life. President Lincoln had asked Bud to come to the funeral but he was so distraught at seeing his beloved friend lying in his coffin that he collapsed and had to be carried home and was ill for days afterward in the throes of inconsolable grief.

In June 1862 Mrs. Taft, Julia and the boys went to live with their maternal grandmother Mrs. Mary Cook (August 5, 1798 - October 23, 1880) in Sag Harbor, Long Island, New York. It is assumed Bud completed his schooling there and graduated ca: 1865.

Very little is known about Bud's adult life as he appeared to move around a lot, a solitary wanderer trying to deal with his traumatic loss. We will never know what the long-term effect was on Bud's psyche watching, as a sensitive, artistic 15-year-old adolescent, his beloved little friend suffer so terribly and die before his eyes.

Bud turns up in the 1870 Census living in Kittery, York County, Maine working as a "captain's clerk" which verifies what was later listed on his death certificate as "previous occupation seaman" He does not show up anywhere on the 1880 Census as he very well may have been at sea. The 1890 Census was destroyed by fire and his is not listed in the 1900 Census. He next turns up in the 1910 Census living in Guilford, Winnebago County, Illinois and finally is listed in the Rockford, Illinois City Directory living at 1126 Crosby Street in the rooming house of Mrs. John Molander and previously had been working as an "office man" [clerk?].

Bud had been under the care of one Dr. H. B. Bailey of 514 E. State Street in Rockford for treatment of Bright's Disease [diabetes] from October 31, 1914 till he developed pneumonia New Year's Day 1915 and died about 2:30 p.m. January 6 in a taxicab on his way to St. Anthony Hospital. He was 67. Mrs. Molander was in the vehicle with Bud and following his collapse and death when about half the distance to the hospital had been traversed, she had the body taken to the Marsh Undertaking Rooms. Bud's remains were shipped to Sag Harbor, Long Island, New York where he was buried in Oakland Cemetery January 9th and rests near his parents and brothers. Bud's tombstone, however, has an incorrect date of birth "January 13th" [confused with his fathers which was the 13th of January] when it was actually January 15th. Only

Julia who married the Rev. John S. Bayne in May 1869 and wrote the memoir *Tad Lincoln's Father* in the 1920s about her time in Washington and the Lincoln's is buried elsewhere. She died at age 88 on December 14, 1933 in Champaign, Illinois.

Like Willie's other best friend Henry Remann, Bud never married.

Notes to Afterword

1. Baptismal record of the Lyons, New York Grace Episcopal Church, March 1, 1847 verifies that Horatio Nelson Taft, Jr. was born January 15, 1847.

2. Willie's severe bout with scarlet fever was reported in a brief article, "The Parent and the Politician" published in the *Chicago Press and Tribune* June 29, 1860 although it had the wrong brother and his age was listed incorrectly. It was Willie and he was nine. "We regret to hear that Mr. Lincoln's [youngest] child, a remarkably bright boy of [six] years of age, is lying ill at the point of death, of scarlet fever…" Although Willie was not "lying ill at the point of death" it was an eerie portent of what would happen two years later.

3. Wayne C. Temple, *Abraham Lincoln From Skeptic to Scholar*, (Mahomet, Il.: Mayhaven Publishing, 1995), 183, "There was strong evidence that three of the Lincoln children were tubercular."

4. *The Diary of Horatio Nelson Taft, 1861 -1865*, Wednesday, January 15, 1862.
   [Bud's 15th birthday]. "Small pox and Typhoid fever are both pre-vailing to a great extent."

5. IBID, 4., Friday, January 17, 1862. "…all fearing the small pox, Julia has been re-vaccinated, the rest of us will be."

6. IBID, 4., Sunday, January 26, 1862. "The two Lincoln boys were here after our boys to go up there [Executive Mansion] to see [their] new pony."

7. Elizabeth Keckley, *Behind The Scenes*, (Urbana, University of Illinois Press, 2004 reprint), 98. Mrs. Keckly [correct spelling] reports that Willie had taken to riding his new pony in the changeable weather and came down with a severe cold.

8. William Seale, *The President's House, Vol. 1*. Washington: White House Historical Association, 1986). 199-200, 379. "Drinking water installed in lower levels but Potomac River water for washing only on 2nd floor living quarters."

9. Ernest G. Furgurson, *Freedom Rising* (New York, Knopf, 2004), 157. "Drinking water For the 2nd floor did not arrive till 1863."

10. Ervin Chapman, *Latest Light on Abraham Lincoln, Vol. 2* (New York, Fleming H. Revell, 1917), 505. "On account of the nature of the disease (varioloid) his (Willie's) Funeral was as private as possible."

11. IBID, 3, 18, "Since the words varioloid and smallpox created panic…"

12. American Medical Association, *Home Medical Encyclopedia, Vol. 2* (New York: Random House, 1989. "variola [varioloid], normally a non-fatal small pox strain often caused by a slight reaction to being re-vaccinated."

13. IBID, 13 "…symptoms of small pox."

14. IBID. 13 "…symptoms of typhoid."

15. IBID, 13 "…symptoms of pneumonia."

Notes to Willie Lincoln's Best Friends

1. *Illinois State Register,* February 27, 1920, 7. Obituary of Henry Remann.

2. *Illinois State Journal*, November 15, 1931. "One afternoon Henry went to the Lincoln Home…"

3. 1910 Springfield High School yearbook *The Capitoline*, "Alumni 1866," Henry Remann and Edward McClernand.

4. Death certificate for Henry Remann, State of Illinois, "lobar pneumonia and heart failure cause of death."

5. IBID, 1,7, Continued obituary.

6. Cemetery records, Wood Lawn Cemetery, Wellsville, Allegany County, New York. Edward Rathbun, Sr., Edward Rathbun, Jr., James Miner Rathbun.

7. Bonnie E. Paull & Richard E. Hart, *Lincoln's Springfield Neighbors* (Charleston, South Carolina, The History Press, 2016), 57. "In 1856, Hannah Rathbun, a widow with two sons, Edward and James, moved to Springfield to live with her brother and sister-in-law, the Reverend Noyes W. Miner. The Miners were renting the Lushbaugh house directly across from the Lincolns."

8. Letter from Mary Lincoln to Hannah (Miner) Rathbun Shearer dated November 20, 1864, "...doubtless our angel boys are re-united [in heaven] as they loved each other so much on earth."

9. Baptisms, Lyons, New York. Grace Episcopal Church, March 1, 1847. Birth and baptismal records for Bud and Julia Taft.

10. Enrollment records of the Lyons Union School year ending March 1854. Bud in First Grade, Julia in Second.

11. *Sag Harbor [New York] Express*, April 19, 1888. Obituary of Horatio Nelson Taft, Sr. "...appointed Chief Examiner in the United States Patent Office."

12. Rockford [Illinois] Morning Star, January 7, 1915, 3. Obituary of Horatio N. Taft, Jr., "...died at 2:30 yesterday afternoon in a taxicab..."

13. Death certificate for Horatio N. Taft, Jr. State of Illinois, "pneumonia and diabetes cause of death."

14. Burials in Oakland Cemetery, Sag Harbor, New York, Sag Harbor Historical Society.

Willie's actual letters in chronological order.

DEAR FRIEND: I WILL
WRITE YOU A FEW LINES TO LET YOU KNOW HOW I AM
GETTING ALONG. I AM PRETTY WELL. THE ROADS ARE
DRYING UP. IT IS SUNDAY AND A PLEASANT DAY.
I HAVEN'T ANYMORE TO SAY SO I MUST BRING
MY LETTER TO AN END.

Wm. W. LINCOLN

THE END.

* Note: Stains on letter are from chocolate bon-bons that Willie
had been eating and then placed the letter in the box
where it was found years later,

very fine here in this town. We saw the
Exhibition on wednesday before last.

Your Truly

Willie Gordon

Dear Henry

This
town is a very beautiful place. Me
and father went to two theatres the
other night. Me and father have a nice
little room to ourselves. We have two
little pitchers on a washstand. The smallest
lled one for me the largest one for
father. We have two little towels
on a top of both pitchers. The smallest
one for me, the largest one for father.

We have two little beds in the
room. The smallest one for me, the
largest one for father.

We have two little wash basins
The smallest one for me, the largest
one for father. The weather is very

Master Henry Remann,

Springfield,

Sangamon Co,

Illinois

Executive man. Washington D.C. May 3, 1861.

Dear henry,

I am sorry
I have not wrote to you at all, since I left you all.
I told My brother bob in my last letter
that there was at least ten thousand soldiers
stationed at the capitol building. I suppose
that you did not learn that Colonel, E. E.
Elsworth had gone to New-york and or=
ganized a regiment—divided into company's,
and brought them here, & to be sworn in—I
doat know when. Some people call them
the b. boys, & others call them, the firemen.

Yours respectfully,

Willie

Lincoln.

Washington, D.C. May 25th/

Dear Alwry

You requested
a letter, & here it is. I want you to give my respects
to Edward McClernand, and tell him this! I feel
very sorry about his mother, and one more thing.
Colonel E. E. Ellsworth went over to Alexandria, Va,
and determined to take the secession flag down of the
Marshall house. So he rushed up the steps untill he
reached the pole, took down the flag, wrapped it around
him [3 men with him], and coming down the steps [his
comrade Brownell being in front of him] Jackson [a se-
cessionist] behind him shot him, immediately his [
Brownell's comrade] shot & killed Jackson.

Your truly
William Lincoln.

From the President of the United States
Jno. G. Nicolay
Priv. Sec.

Master Henry Remann,

Springfield,
Sangamon C.
Illinois.

care of [ ]
[ ]

Dear Edward

I am exceed—
ingly anxious to know, how you, and the
rest of the boys are getting along. I have
been quite well ever since, I left you.
(Today being Wednesday), Mother thinks
of leave on friday morning at 6, o,
clock. Our expected destination is
probably Newport R. I. The reason
for this is, that our journey will
last only a few days now, it will
be all the same as if we had not
been any where but here. You
cannot imagine, how nice it is to see
the people bathing at the beach,
now near by.

                              from
                       your friend & play—mate
                              Willie
                       Lincoln

Washington, D.C. September 30/64
Executive Mansion

Dear Henry,
            The last letter you sent
to me, arrived in due time, which
was on Saturday. My companions
and I are raising a battalion. When
I came here, I would until the be-
:ginning of ____, and then joined
another boy in trying to get up
a regiment. We failed however,
and I then attempted to muster
a company. That drew broke up.
Thereafter a boy stated he com-
:manded a battalion, and my
company and I at once joined,
believing that he spoke the
truth, but we found out that
such was not the case. Disap:

; pointed in every way we
set to work and raised one,
which is in a high state of effi-
ciency and discipline.
I am
Dear Henry
Yours sincerely
William W. Lincoln

Transcriptions of Willie's Letters 1859-1861

(Transcriptions with his exact length of lines, spelling and punctuation where he uses " and = instead of - to divide words at end of lines. I only inserted missing or illegible words)

Springfield April24,
1859

Dear Friend   I will
write you a few lines to let you know how I am
getting along. I am pretty well The roads are
drying up it is Sunday and a pleasant day
I have not any more to say
so I must bring
my letter to an end

Wm W Lincoln

The end.

*This letter is stained with chocolate, but by holding a scan of it up to the light I was able for the first time to decipher the missing words. The person who found this letter is Miss Hannah Adele Rathbun (October 3, 1880 - June 26, 1979), who was the daughter of James Miner Rathbun (1852/3 - August 5, 1898), brother of Willie's friend Edward "Eddie" Rathbun, Jr. (1848 - 1862), asserts that "it [the letter] was kept in the same box with a bon-bon he [Willie] gave my uncle that was taken from a banquet given for the Prince of Wales at the White House." However, (1) The Prince of Wales visited the White House in 1860 during the Buchanan administration before Willie was even in Washington. And, (2) it was written in Springfield *April 24, 1859 and sent to Eddie, who had recently moved with his family to Wellsboro, Pennsylvania. Hannah Rathbun Shearer lived in Springfield from 1856-59 with her husband Dr. John Shearer and sons Eddie and James who were friends with Willie and Tad so it simply may be her memory was faulty as she (Hannah Adele Rathbun) lived to be 99.

*Mary Lincoln wrote a letter to Hannah Shearer the same day. The two were mailed together.

6th 1859

Chicago Springfield of June

Dear Henry:

This
town is a very beautiful place.   Me
and father went to two theatres the
other night.   Me and father have a nice
little room to ourselves. We have two lit
tle pitcher[s] on a washstand.   The smal
lest one for me, the largest one for
father.   We have two little towels
one on top of both pitchers   The smallest
one for me,   the largest one for father
                    We have two little beds in the
    room.   The smallest one for me, the
    largest one for father.
                    We have two little wash basins,
    The smallest one for me, the largest
    one for father. The weather is very
    fine here, in this town. Was [at] this
    Exhibition on Wednesday before last.
                    Yours Truly,
                    Willie Lincoln

*Willie wrote this letter possibly modeled on the fairy tale "The Three
Bears," at the Tremont House Hotel in Chicago where he and his father
were staying. Coincidentally, Stephen Douglas was also staying there
that week. *Chicago Press and Tribune*, June 8, 1859, 1. "Both Hon.
Abraham Lincoln and Senator Douglas are in town, and stopping at
the Tremont."

Executive man Washington D.C. May 3, 1861.
Dear henry,

                              I am sorry
I have not wrote to you at all, since I left youall.
   I told my brother bob in my last letter
that there was at least tem thousand soldiers
stationed at the Capitol building. I suppose
that you did not learn that Colonel E.E.
Elsworth had gone to New York and or=
ganized a Regiment, =divided into company's,
and brought them here, & to be sworn in=
I don't know when. Some people call them
the B. boy's & others call them,
the firemen.

                   Yours respectfully,
                        Willie
                           Lincoln.

Washington, D.C. May 25/61

Dear Henry

You request
a letter, & here it is. I want you to give my respects
to Edward McClernand, and tell him that I feel
very sorry about his mother, and one more thing.
Colonel E.E. Ellsworth went over to Alexandria, Va.
and determined to take the secession flag down of[f]
the Marshall house. So he rushed up the steps untill he
reached the pole, took down the flag, wrapped it around
him [8 men with him], and coming down the steps [his
comrade Brownell, being in front of him] and Jackson a se=
cessionists] behind him, shot him, immediately his [
ellsworths] comrades] went & killed Jackson.

Yours truly,
Willie Lincoln.

*Note, Willie put in brackets himself in this letter except after of[f]
that I inserted.

172

S. LAIRD
MANSION HOUSE
Long Branch, N.J. August 21, 1861

Dear Edward

I am exceed=
ingly anxious to know, how you, and the
rest of the boys are getting along. I have
been quite well ever since, I left you.
(Today being Wednesday), Mother thinks
of leave[ing] on friday morning at 6,o.
clock. Our expected destination is
probably Newport R.I. The reason
for this is, that our journey will
last only a few days now, it will
be all the same as if we had not
been any where but here. You
cannot imagine, how nice it is to see
the people bathing at the beach,
isso near by.
from
your friend & play=mate
Willie
Lincoln

*Some scholars think the Edward Willie is writing to is Edward
McCauley. I think it is Edward McClernand, Willie's friend back in
Springfield.

..

Washington, D,C, September 30/1861
Executive Mansion

Dear Henry,

The last letter you sent
me, arrived in due time, which
was on Saturday. My companions
and I are raising a battalion.   When
I came here, I waited until the be:
ginning of June, and then joined
w[ith] another boy in trying to get up
a regiment. We failed however,
and I then attempted to muster
a Company. That soon broke up.
Thereafter a boy stated he com:
manded a battalion, and my
Company and I at once joined,
believing that he spoke the
truth, but we found out that
such was not the case. Disap:
pointed in every way we
set to work and raised one,
which is in a high state of effi:
ciency and discipline.
I am
Dear Henry
Yours sincerely
William W. Lincoln

WILLIE'S LETTERS - CREDITS

1. Willie to Edward "Eddie" Rathbun, Jr. from Springfield April 24, 1859 - Abraham Lincoln Presidential Library and Museum (ALPLM).

2. Willie to Henry Remann from Chicago June 6, 1859 - Special Collections Research Center, University of Chicago Library.

3. Willie to Henry Remann from Washington May 3, 1861 - Abraham Lincoln Presidential Library and Museum (ALPLM).

4. Willie to Henry Remann from Washington May 23, 1861 - Abraham Lincoln Presidential Library and Museum (ALPLM).

5. Willie to Edward McClernand from Long Branch, NJ August 21, 1861 -Abraham Lincoln Presidential Library and Museum (ALPLM).

6. Willie to Henry Remann from Washington September 30, 1861 - Abraham Lincoln Presidential Library and Museum (ALPLM).

BIBLIOGRAPHY

BOOKS AND PERIODICALS
PRIMARY SOURCES

Ayres, Philip Wheelock. "Lincoln As Neighbor." *Review of Reviews* (February 1918).

Basler, Roy P., ed. *Collected Works of Abraham Lincoln,* New Brunswick, NJ, Rutgers U. Press, 1953. 9 v.

Bayne, Julia (Taft). *Tad Lincoln's Father,* Lincoln, University of Nebraska Press, 2001. 89p. Orig. 1931.

Bayne, Julia (Taft). "Willie and Tad Lincoln." *St. Nicholas.* (February 1897), p. 277-282.

Beale, Howard K., ed. *The Diary of Edward Bates 1859-1866,* Washington D.C., U.S. Govt. Printing Office, 1933. 685 p.

Boyden, Ann L. *War Reminisces, or Echoes from Hospital and White House,* Boston, D. Lothrop, 1887. 250 p.

Brooks, Noah. *Washington in Lincoln's Time,* New York, Rinehart, 1958, 309 p. Orig. 1895.

Browne, Frances Fisher. *Everyday Life of Abraham Lincoln,* Chicago, Ill., Browne & Howell, 1914. 622 p. Orig. 1886..

Browning, Orville Hickman. *The Diary of Orville Hickman Browning, Vol. 1,1850-1864,* Springfield, (Collections of the Illinois State Historical Library), 1925, Vol. XX, Lincoln Series, Vol. II. p 553.

Bugbee, Emily. *The Little Corporal,* (July 1865) p. 11.

Burlingame, Michael, ed., *With Lincoln in the White House: Letters, Memoranda, and Other Writings of John Nicolay,* Carbondale, Ill., Southern Illinois University Press, 2000. 274 p.

Burlingame, Michael & Ettlinger, John R. Turner, ed., *Inside Lincoln's White House; The Complete Civil of Diary of John Hay,* Carbondale, Ill., 1999. 293 p.

Burlingame, Michael, ed., *John Hay's Civil War Correspondence and Selected Writings,* Carbondale, Ill., Southern Illinois University Press, 2000. 294 p.

Carpenter, Francis B. *Inner Life of Abraham Lincoln: Six Months in the White House,* Lincoln, University of Nebraska Press, 1995. 295 p. Orig. 1866.

Dyba, Thomas & Painter, George L. *Seventeen Years at Eighth and Jackson,* Lisle, IL, IBC Publications, 1985. 68p.

Grimsley, Elizabeth (Todd). "Six Months in the White House," Journal of the Illinois State Historical Society, Vol. xix, nos. 3-4. (Oct.-Jan. 1926-27), p. 68-69.

Gurley, Rev. Phineas T. "Unfinished Manuscript," ca. 1866.

Hertz, Emanuel, *The Hidden Lincoln,* New York, Viking, 1938. 461 p.

Keckley, Elizabeth. *Behind the Scenes,* New York, Oxford U. Press, 1988. 371p.

Lamon, Ward Hill, *Life of Abraham Lincoln,* James & Osgood, 1872. 547 p.

Lamon, Ward Hill, *Recollections of Abraham Lincoln,* ed by Dorothy Lamon Teillard. Chicago, A.C. McClurg, 1895. 276 p.

Lancaster County Historical Society, Lancaster PA, "Bills of Sale [of slaves, etc.]. William Porter to Nicholas Boyd August 11, 1800 and William Porter to Andrew Porter July 26, 1785." African American Records Collection 1780-1984, Pennsylvania Slavery Sources, Reference nos. 112, 113, p 3-4.

Miers, Earl S., ed. *Lincoln Day by Day, A Chronology 1809-1865*, Dayton, OH, Morningside, 1991. 487p.

Ostendorf, Lloyd. *Lincoln's Photographs, A Complete Album*, Dayton OH, Rockywood Press, 1998. 437 p.

Ostendorf, Lloyd and Oleksy, Walter, eds. *Lincoln's Unknown Private Life: An Oral History by his Black Housekeeper Mariah (Bartlett) Vance 1850-1860*, Mamaroneck, NY, Hastings House 1995. 260p.

Paull, Bonnie E. & Hart, Richard E. *Lincoln's Springfield Neighborhood*, Charleston, Sc, History Press, 2015. 219 p.

Pendel, Thomas F. *Thirty-Six Years in the White House*, Washington, D.C., Neale Pub. Co. , 1902. 176 p.

Power, John Carroll. *Abraham Lincoln, His life, Public Services, Death and Great Funeral Cortege with a History and Description of the National Lincoln Monument,* Springfield, H.W. Rokker, 1889. n. p. Orig. 1872.

Sangamon County Historical Society.

Shakespeare, William. *King John*, New York, Cambridge Univ. Press, 1984. 188 p. Orig. ca: 1599.

Springfield High School. *Capitoline Yearbook 1910,* "Alumni," p. 35.

Stoddard, William O. *Inside the White House in War Times*, New York, C.L. Webster, 1880. 244 p.

Taft, Sr., Horatio Nelson. *The Civil War Diary of Horatio Nelson Taft 1861-65*, Washington, D.C., 1865. n. p., unpublished, online at American History.

Turner, Justin & Turner, Levitt, Linda, eds. *Mary Todd Lincoln: Her Life and Letters*, New York, Knopf, 1972. 750 p.

Washington, John E. *They Knew Lincoln,* New York, Dutton, 1942. 244 p.

Williams, C.S., comp. *Williams Springfield Directory, City Guide and Business Mirror for 1860-61,* Springfield, Johnson & Bradford, 1860.

Willis, Nathaniel Parker. "Willie Lincoln." *Home Journal.* (March 1862)

Wilson, Douglas L. & Davis, Rodney, eds. *Herndon's Informants,* Urbana, University of Illinois Press, 1998. 827 p.

SECONDARY SOURCES

Adleman, Gary E. & Richter, John J, eds. *99 Historical Images of Civil War Washington*, Oldsmar, FL, The Center for Civil War Photography, 2006. 32p.

Algeo, Matthew. *Abe and Fido: Lincoln's Love of Animals and the Touching Story of his Favorite Canine Companion, Chicago,* Chicago Review Press, 2015. 176 p.

Angle, Paul M. *Here I Have Lived: A History of Lincoln's Springfield. 1821-1865.* Springfield, IL, Abraham Lincoln Association, 1936. 313 p.

Baker, Jean H. *Mary Todd Lincoln,* New York, Norton, 1987. 429 p.

Barton William E. *Life of Abraham Lincoln*, Indianapolis, Bobbs-Merrill, 1925. 2 v.

Belanger, Jeff. *Who's Haunting the White House?,* New York, Sterling, 2008. 56 p.

Beveridge, Albert J. *Abraham Lincoln 1809-1858, Vol. 2*, London, Glance, 1928. 2 v.

Brown, Virginia Stuart. *Through Lincoln's Door*, Springfield, Li-Co Art & Letter Service, 1952. 84 p.

Bullard, F. Laurelton. *Tad and His Father,* Boston, Little, Brown 1915, 102 p.

Burlingame, Michael. *Inner World of Abraham Lincoln*, Urbana, IL, University of Illinois Press, 1994. 380p.

Chapman, Ervin S. *Latest Light on Abraham Lincoln Vol. 2,* New York, Fleming H. Revell, 1917. 2 v. 570p.

Current, Richard. *The Lincoln Nobody Knows*, Madison, Lincoln Fellowship of Wisconsin, 1958. 22 p

Donald, David Herbert. *Lincoln*, New York, Simon & Schuster, 1995. 714p.

Donald, David Herbert. *Lincoln At Home*, New York, Simon & Schuster, 2000. 124p.

Dubois, Charlotte A. "Willie Lincoln as Boy of Letters." *The Power of the Written Word,* 1922.

Evans, William A. *Mrs. Abraham Lincoln*, New York, Knopf, 1932. 364p.

Ferguson, Andrew. *Land of Lincoln*, New York, Atlantic Monthly Press, 2007. 279p.

Fergurson, Ernest B. *Freedom Rising*, New York, Knopf, 2004. 363p.

Fleischner, Jennifer. *Mrs. Lincoln and Mrs. Keckly*, New York, Broadway Books, 2003. 372p.

Forman, Stephen M. *A Guide to Civil War Washington,* Washington, D.C., Elliot &Clark, 2002. 208p.

Fuller, Frank A. "A Day With the Lincoln Family," Abraham Lincoln Presidential Library and Museum (ALPLM), Monaghan, 1458.

Goff, John S. *Robert T. Lincoln: A Man in His Own Right*, Norman, University of Oklahoma Press, 1969. 286p.

Hambly, Barbara. *The Emancipator's Wife*, New York, Bantam, 2005. 608p.

Helm, Katharine. *True Story of Mary, Wife of Lincoln*, New York, Harper, 1923. 309p.

Herndon, William H. & Weik, Jesse W. *Herndon's Lincoln*, Urbana, IL, University of Illinois Press, 2006. 481p. Orig. 1888.

Holien, K.B. *Battle of Ball's Bluff*, Orange, VA, Moss Publication, 1985. 166p

Kimmel, Stanley M. *Mr. Lincoln's Washington*, New York, Coward-McCann, 1957. 224p.

Kunhardt, Dorothy Meserve & Philip B. Kunhardt., Jr., *Twenty Days,* Secaucus, NJ, Castle Books, 1993. Orig. 1965.

Kunhardt, Dorothy Meserve. ",,, and his face was chalky white." Show Magazine, (January 1963), p. 87-91,

Kunhardt, Dorothy (Meserve). "Willie Was the Favorite." n. d.

Leech, Margaret. *Reveille in Washington, 1860-1865*, Westport, CT, Greenwood Press, 1971. 483 p. Orig. 1941.

Longstreth, Thomas M. *Tad Lincoln, the President's Son*, Philadelphia, Westminster Pres 1944. 263 p.

Luthin, Reinhard H. *The Real Abraham Lincoln*, Englewood Cliffs, NJ, Prentice-Hall, 1960. 778p.

McBride, Robert. *Personal Recollections of Abraham Lincoln*, Indianapolis, IN, Bobbs-Merrill, 1926. 78p.

Motier, Donald. *Mystic Chords of Memory: The Lost Journal of Abraham Lincoln*, Bloomington, IN, Xlibris, 2012. 204.p.

Motier, Donald. "Mortality of Willie Lincoln Re-visited." unpublished manuscript, Harrisburg, PA, 2015.

Neely, Mark E., ed. *Abraham Lincoln Encyclopedia,* New York, McGraw-Hill, 1982. 156p.

Neely, Mark E. *Last Best Hope of Earth*, Cambridge, Mass., Harvard University Press, 1993. 214p.

Neely, Jr., Mark E. & Holzer, Harold. *The Lincoln Family Album*, Carbondale , Ill., Southern Illinois University Press, 1990. 161 p.

Nicolay, John & Hay, John. *Abraham Lincoln: A History*, New York, Century, 1890. 10 vols.

Packard, Jerrold M. *The Lincolns in the White House*, New York, St. Martin's, 2005. 290p.

Paull, Bonnie E. & Hart, Richard E. *Lincoln's Springfield Neighborhood*, Charleston, SC, History Press, 2015. 219p.

Randall, James G. *Lincoln the President*. New York, Dodd, Mead, 1945. 4 v.

Randall, James G. *Mr. Lincoln*, New York, Dodd, Mead, 1957. 392 p.

Randall, Ruth Painter. *Colonel Elmer Ellsworth*, Boston, Little, Brown, 1960. 295p.

Randall, Ruth Painter. *Lincoln's Animal Friends*. Boston, Little, Brown, 1958.152 p.

Randall, Ruth Painter. *Lincoln's Sons*, Boston, Litle Brown, 1955. 373 p.

Sandburg, Carl. *Abraham Lincoln: The Prairie Years*, New York, Dell, 1960. 320p. Orig. 1926, 2 vols.

Sandburg., Carol. *Abraham Lincoln: The War Years, 1861-1865*, New York, Dell, 1960. 443p. Orig. 1939, 4 vols.

Sandburg, Carl & Angle, Paul. *Mary Lincoln, Wife and Widow*, New York, Harcourt-Brace, 1932. 357p.

Seale, William. *The President's House, A History*, Washington, D.C., White House Historical Association, 2 v., 1986. 1224 p.

Shenk, Joshua Wolf. *Lincoln's Melancholy*, Boston, Houghton-Mifflin, 2005. 350p.

Shutes, Milton H. *Lincoln and the Doctors*, New York, Pioneer Press, 1933. 152p.

Shutes, Milton H. *Lincoln's Emotional Life*, Philadelphia, Dorrance, 1957. 222p.

Shutes, Milton H. "Mortality of the Five Lincoln Boys." *Lincoln Herald*, vol. 57, (Spring-Summer) 1955.

Stephenson, Nathaniel W. *Lincoln, An Account of His Personal Life*, London, Hutchinson, 1924. 352p.

Tarbell, Ida M. *Life of Abraham Lincoln*, New York, Lincoln Memorial Assoc., 1900. 2 v., 475p.

Temple, Wayne C. *Abraham Lincoln: From Skeptic to Prophet*, Mahomet, IL, Mayhaven, Pub., 1995. 446 p.

Temple, Wayne C. *Alexander Williamson, Friend of the Lincolns*, Racine, WI, Lincoln Fellowship of Wisconsin, 1997. 48 p.

Temple, Wayne C. *By Square and Compass, Saga of the Lincoln Home*, Mahomet, IL, Mayhaven Pub., 2002. 321p.

Tripp, C. A. *Intimate World of Abraham Lincoln*, New York, Free Press, 2005. 343 p.

Warren, Dr. Louis A. "Three Generations of Lincoln Boys." *Lincoln Lore*, no. 244 (Dec. 11, 1933). p. 1.

Weaver, John D. *Tad Lincoln, Mischief Maker in the White House*, New York, Dodd, Mead, 1963. 145 p..

Weik, Jesse W. *The Real Lincoln*, New York, Houghton-Mifflin, 1922. 323p.

Whitcomb, John & Claire. *Real Life in the White House,* New York, Routledge, 2000. 511p.

Williams, Mathilde D. "Why Willie Lincoln Was Temporarily Placed in the Carroll Vault, Oak Hill Cemetery, Georgetown, D.C." unpublished manuscript, Martin Luther King, Jr. Memorial Library, Washington, D.C., 1962. 6 p.

Wilson, Rufus Rockwell, ed. *Intimate Memories of Lincoln*, Elmira, NY, Primavera Press, 1945. 629p.

Wilson, Rufus Rockwell, ed. *Lincoln Among His Friends*, Caldwell, ID, Caxton Publishers, Ltd., 1942. 506 p.

LIST OF CREDITS FOR PHOTOGRAPHS, AND MISCELLANEA

1. Front cover. William "Willie" Wallace Lincoln colorized photo courtesy of the author

2. Willie Lincoln about age 4 Springfield ca. 1855 - Library of Congress.

3. Copy of page from Niagara Falls [Ontario] Museum Guestbook for July 1857 showing "A. Lincoln and Family" and "P. T. Barnum." - Courtesy of the Niagara Falls Museum.

4. Willie about age 8 Springfield ca. 1859 - Courtesy of the Allen Public Library, Fort Wayne, IN #3759.

5. Willie, Mary and Tad Lincoln Springfield, ca.. 1859 - Chicago History Museum.

6. Willie with lock of his hair and daguerreotype ,Springfield ca. 1859 - Abraham Lincoln Presidential Library & Museum (ALPLM).

7. Tremont Hotel, Chicago pre-1871, where Willie and Abe stayed June 1859. - Chicago History Museum.

8. Mary (Todd) Lincoln's invitation to Willie's 9ᵗʰ Birthday party, - Abraham Lincoln Presidential Library & Museum (ALPLM).

9. Willie age 9 Springfield 1860. - Chicago History Museum.

10. Springfield home of the Lincolns', summer 1860 with Willie and Tad (behind post). - Courtesy of the Allen Public Library, Fort Wayne, IN #4018.

11. Springfield home with crowd in front August 8, 1860; Willie is at 2ⁿᵈ floor window, 2ⁿᵈ from left. - Library of Congress.

12. Dr. William S. Wallace, Willie's namesake and uncle, Springfield. - Courtesy of the Allen Public Library, Ft. Wayne, IN #3997.

13. Henry Christian Remann, Willie's best friend in Springfield, ca. 1861. - Courtesy of the Allen Public Library, Fort Wayne, IN

14. Grave stone of Edward "Eddie" Rathbun, Jr., his brother James Miner Rathbun, sister-in-law and niece, Wood Lawn Cemetery, Wellsville, NY - Courtesy of the Allegany County Historical Society.

15. Fido, the Lincoln dog, Springfield, April 1865. - Courtesy of the Allen Public, Ft. Wayne, IN..

16. Jones House, Harrisburg, PA, ca. 1860s where Mary, Willie & Tad stayed over on the afternoon and night of February 22, 23, 1861 on way to Washington. - The Historical Society of Dauphin County [Harrisburg, PA].

17. Elizabeth Keckly - Courtesy of the Allen Public Library, Fort Wayne, IN #3189.

18. South view of White House 1861. Possibly Willie sitting on wall at right. - National Archives.

19. Horatio "Bud" Nelson Taft, Jr. & Halsey "Holly" Cook Taft, ca. 1859-60, Willie's best friends in Washington. - *Tad Lincoln's Father* by Julia (Bayne) Taft.

20. Julia Taft, Washington, ca. 1861 - *Tad Lincoln's Father* by Julia (Taft) Bayne.

21. Willie's circus 'Programme" - *Tad Lincoln's Father* by Julia (Taft) Bayne.

22. Colonel Elmer Ellsworth, Washington, ca. 1861. National Archives.

23. Colonel Edward D. Baker, ca. 1861 - Courtesy of the Allen Public Library, Ft. Wayne, IN, #4639.

24. Abraham Lincoln, Washington, ca. June 1861 - Abraham Lincoln Presidential Library & Museum (ALPLM).

25. Willie, age 10, Tad and Uncle Lockwood Todd, Brady Studio, Washington, April 1861. - Abraham Presidential Library & Museum (ALPLM)

26. Willie holding Uncle Lockwood Todd's walking stick, Brady Studio, Washington, April 1861. - Abraham Lincoln Presidential Library & Museum (ALPLM).

27. Mansion House, Long Branch, New Jersey August 1861 where Willie, Mary and Tad and Eddie, James and Hannah (Rathbun) Shearer vacationed August 24-29, 1861. - Pach Brothers photo. North Jersey Shore Resort Era Collection, Courtesy of the Long Branch Public Library.

28. Abe, Willie & Tad, Christmas 1861, White House - Print by Lloyd Ostendorf. Courtesy of Donna Aschenbrenner.

29. Prince of Wales Room, White House, ca. 1870 where Willie died February 20, 1862. -White House Historical Association.

30. William Thomas Carroll Tomb, Oak Hill Cemetery, Georgetown where Willie lay from February 24, 1862 - April 20, 1865. - Courtesy of the author.

31. Carroll Tomb floor showing drag marks - Courtesy of the author.

32. Willie and Lincoln's flower-draped coffins resting in temporary vault, Oak Ridge Cemetery, Springfield, May 5, 1865 - Abraham Lincoln Presidential Library & Museum (ALPLM).

33. Willie & Eddie's crypt, Lincoln Tomb, Springfield. - Courtesy of the author.

34. General Andrew Christy Porter, Harrisburg Cemetery, Harrisburg, PA - Courtesy of the author.

35. Back cover. The author wearing replica Union uniform of his great-grandfather Sgt. Charles MacNair Powers at his grave, Greenwood Cemetery, Lancaster, PA. - Courtesy of the author.

Newspapers

Chicago Press and Tribune

Chicago Daily News

Constitutional Union (Washington , D.C.)

Evening Star (Washington, D.C.)

Illinois State Register

Illinois State Journal

National Intelligencer (Washington, D.C.)

National Republican (Washington, D.C.)

New Republic (Washington, D.C.)

New York Herald

New York Times

New York World

Niagara Falls Gazette

Rockford Morning Star (Illinois)

Sag Harbor Express (New York)

Star Gazette (Elmira, New York)

State Journal Register (Springfield, Illinois)

ADDENDA

1. Family Tree of Donald Motier, a.k.a. Donald William Miller, showing relationship to Mary (Todd) Lincoln and William "Willie" Wallace Lincoln, Lite Family Tree Maker CD 2008 by Ancestry.com. and Ancestry.com. 2017.

2. Lancaster County Historical Society, Lancaster, PA ,"Bills of Sales for slaves, etc. William Porter to Nicholas Boyd August 11, 1800 and William Porter to Andrew Porter July 26th, 1785," African American Records Collection 1780 - 1984. Pennsylvania Slavery Sources, Ref. nos. 112-113, p. 3-4.

Relationship: Donald William Miller to William Wallace Lincoln

William Wallace Lincoln is the Third Cousin 2x Removed of Donald William Miller

4th Great Grandfather

General Andrew Christy Porter
b: 24 Sep 1743
Montgomery Co., PA
d: 16 Nov 1813
Harrisburg, PA

3rd Great Grandmother ← *Sisters* → 3rd Great Grand Aunt

Mary Porter *married Nicholas Boyd (1772–1840)*
b: 01 Jan 1781
Philadelphia, PA
d: 08 Mar 1839
Lancaster Co., PA

Elizabeth Rittenhouse Porter
b: 27 Sep 1769
Lancaster Co, PA
d: 21 Jun 1850
Kentucky

2nd Great Grandfather

Stephen William Porter Boyd
b: 09 May 1818
Lancaster Co, PA
d: 20 Jul 1877
Peach Bottom, Lancaster Co., P

First Cousin 4x Removed

Elizabeth Ann Parker
b: May 1795
Kentucky
d: 05 Jul 1825
Kentucky

Great Grandmother

Mary Porter Boyd
b: Aug 1843
Peach Bottom, Lancaster Co, PA
d: 20 May 1900
Lancaster, PA

Second Cousin 3x Removed

Mary Ann Parker Todd Lincoln
b: 13 Dec 1818
Kentucky
d: 16 Jul 1882
Springfield, Illinois

Grandmother

Ella May Powers
b: 20 May 1887
Lancaster, PA
d: 12 Oct 1934
Harrisburg, PA

Third Cousin 2x Removed

William Wallace Lincoln
b: 21 Dec 1850
Springfield, Illinois
d: 20 Feb 1862
Washington DC

Father

Donald Boyd Miller
b: 03 Oct 1908
Harrisburg, PA
d: 17 Sep 1990
Harrisburg, PA

Self

Donald William Miller
b: 17 May 1943
Harrisburg, Pennsylvania
d:

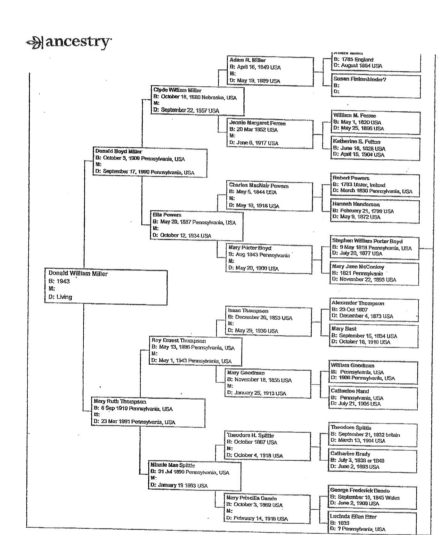

⊰⊱ancestry·

Donald William Miller
B: 1943
M:
D: Living

Donald Boyd Miller
B: October 3, 1908 Pennsylvania, USA
M:
D: September 17, 1990 Pennsylvania, USA

Clyde William Miller
B: October 18, 1880 Nebraska, USA
M:
D: September 22, 1957 USA

Adam R. Miller
B: April 16, 1849 USA
M:
D: May 19, 1889 USA

JOSEPH MILLER
B: 1785 England
D: August 1854 USA

Susan Finkenbinder?
B:
D:

Jennie Margaret Ferree
B: 20 Mar 1852 USA
M:
D: June 6, 1917 USA

William M. Ferree
B: May 1, 1820 USA
D: May 25, 1895 USA

Katherine S. Felton
B: June 18, 1828 USA
D: April 15, 1904 USA

Ella Powers
B: May 20, 1887 Pennsylvania, USA
M:
D: October 12, 1934 USA

Charles MacNair Powers
B: May 5, 1844 USA
M:
D: May 18, 1918 USA

Robert Powers
B: 1783 Ulster, Ireland
D: March 1850 Pennsylvania, USA

Hannah Henderson
B: February 21, 1799 USA
D: May 9, 1872 USA

Mary Porter Boyd
B: Aug 1843 Pennsylvania
M:
D: May 20, 1900 USA

Stephen William Porter Boyd
B: 9 May 1818 Pennsylvania, USA
D: July 20, 1877 USA

Mary Jane McConkey
B: 1821 Pennsylvania
D: November 22, 1893 USA

Mary Ruth Thompson
B: 6 Sep 1910 Pennsylvania, USA
M:
D: 23 Mar 1991 Pennsylvania, USA

Roy Ernest Thompson
B: May 13, 1886 Pennsylvania, USA
M:
D: May 1, 1943 Pennsylvania, USA

Isaac Thompson
B: December 26, 1853 USA
M:
D: May 29, 1930 USA

Alexander Thompson
B: 23 Oct 1807
D: December 4, 1873 USA

Mary Bast
B: September 15, 1834 USA
D: October 18, 1910 USA

Mary Goodman
B: November 18, 1856 USA
M:
D: January 25, 1913 USA

William Goodman
B: Pennsylvania, USA
D: 1908 Pennsylvania, USA

Catharine Hand
B: Pennsylvania, USA
D: July 21, 1905 USA

Minnie Mae Spittle
B: 31 Jul 1890 Pennsylvania, USA
M:
D: January 19 1963 USA

Theodore H. Spittle
B: October 1867 USA
M:
D: October 4, 1918 USA

Theodore Spittle
B: September 21, 1832 britain
D: March 13, 1904 USA

Catharine Brady
B: July 3, 1839 or 1840
D: June 2, 1893 USA

Mary Priscilla Dando
B: October 3, 1869 USA
M:
D: February 14, 1918 USA

George Frederick Dando
B: September 10, 1845 Wales
D: June 2, 1909 USA

Lucinda Ellen Etter
B: 1839
D: ? Pennsylvania, USA

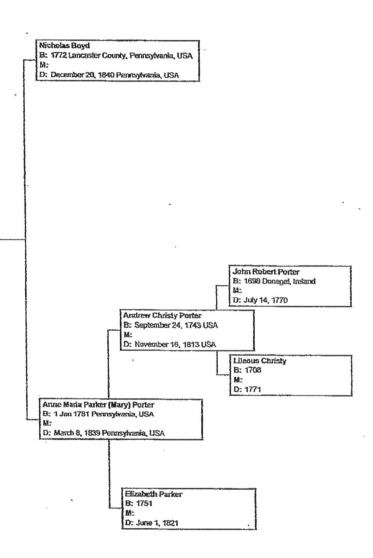

Nicholas Boyd
B: 1772 Lancaster County, Pennsylvania, USA
M:
D: December 20, 1840 Pennsylvania, USA

John Robert Porter
B: 1698 Donegal, Ireland
M:
D: July 14, 1770

Andrew Christy Porter
B: September 24, 1743 USA
M:
D: November 16, 1813 USA

Lileous Christy
B: 1708
M:
D: 1771

Anne Maria Parker (Mary) Porter
B: 1 Jan 1781 Pennsylvania, USA
M:
D: March 8, 1839 Pennsylvania, USA

Elizabeth Parker
B: 1751
M:
D: June 1, 1821

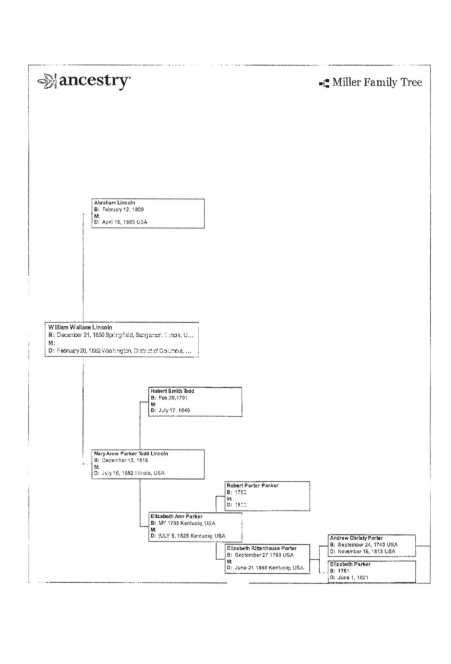

Abraham Lincoln
B: February 12, 1809
M:
D: April 15, 1865 USA

William Wallace Lincoln
B: December 21, 1850 Springfield, Sangamon, Illinois, U...
M:
D: February 20, 1862 Washington, District of Columbia, ...

Robert Smith Todd
B: Feb.25,1791
M:
D: July 17, 1849

Mary Anne Parker Todd Lincoln
B: December 13, 1818
M:
D: July 16, 1882 Illinois, USA

Robert Porter Parker
B: 1760
M:
D: 1800

Elizabeth Ann Parker
B: MY 1795 Kentucky, USA
M:
D: JULY 5, 1825 Kentucky, USA

Elizabeth Rittenhouse Porter
B: September 27 1769 USA
M:
D: June 21 1850 Kentucky, USA

Andrew Christy Porter
B: September 24, 1743 USA
D: November 16, 1813 USA

Elizabeth Parker
B: 1751
D: June 1, 1821

Lancaster County, Pennsylvania Bills of Sale for Slaves

Source: Bill of Sale; William Porter to Nicholas Boyd. Dated 11 August 1800. Documents Case 1, Folder 15, Item 5. Lancaster County Historical Society.
Notes: Transfers ownership of the Negro man Abraham, a brown mare, and various household items, to Nicholas Boyd for 150 pounds in gold or silver coin.

Reference Number: 113

Source: Bill of Sale; William Porter to Andrew Porter. Dated 26 July 1785. Documents Case 1, Folder 13, Item 8. Lancaster County Historical Society.
Notes: Full text of Exemplification, William Porter to Andrew Porter:

> "Know all Men by these Presents that I Wm. Porter of the Township of Little Britain County of Lancaster & State of Pennsylvania for and in Consideration of the sum of four hundred & twenty pounds Lawfull Money of the State aforesaid to me in hand paid

> by Andrew Porter of the Township County & State aforesaid at or before the Sealing and Delivery of these presents the Receipt whereof I the said Wm. Porter do hereby acknowledge Have granted bargained and sold and by these presents Doth grant bargain and sell to the sd. Andrew Porter his heir Executors Administrators or Assigns (Viz.) All my Movable Astate, that is to say one Negroe Man named Abner aged thirty four years one do. named Abbe aged twenty years one do. named Senaca aged fourteen years one Negroe Woman named Fanny aged twenty nine years one Negroe Girl named Reach aged eight years one Negroe Girl named Dark aged five years, one Negroe Woman named Jean aged twenty one years òne Negroe Boy named Ned aged five years and also one Negroe Girl named Peg aged two years also one Negroe Boy named Benn aged four years and one Negroe Woman named Else aged twenty years and the said Els. Child caled Sam, also one brown Gelding aged eight years, also two Mares & one Colt and Seventeen head of horned Cattle, thirty six Sheep, forty hogs, Together with all my household furniture and farming Utentials. . ."
> [Signed William Porter, 26 July 1785.]
> "N.B. One Negroe named Cyrus aged eighteen years which was neglected to be mentioned in the within Bill of Sale, but noted here before Signing and delivering--"

James Jacks, Recorder. Recorded in Deed Book DD, page 268, October 15, 1785. Exemplification made March 17, 1800.

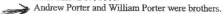

Andrew Porter and William Porter were brothers.

CPSIA information can be obtained
at www.ICGtesting.com
Printed in the USA
BVHW032125290419
546911BV00001B/31/P